'NOT LIKE ANY OTHER HOME'

HERBERT WHITE
AND THE CHILDREN'S HOME & MISSION

BOB HOLMAN

CAMPAIGN LITERATURE
SALTCOATS

Published in Great Britain
by Campaign Literature

First Edition 1994

I.S.B.N. 1 872463 16 9

Printed in Great Britain by
Campaign Literature
Adelaide College
Nineyard Street
Saltcoats
Ayrshire KA21 5HS

Doctor Bob Holman is a former Professor of Social Administration who left university life to be a part of a community project on a council estate in Bath and more recently in Easterhouse, Glasgow. He is a trustee of Mill Grove which grew out of the Children's Home & Mission, started by Herbert White in 1899. The Home has provided care for hundreds of children without ever asking the public for money. Its members have relied completely on God. Its work and the life of Herbert White have been little known and hence Bob Holman has researched and written this book in order to make the story known to a larger audience.

Front Cover Photo: Herbert White as a young man.

To Bruce and Ruth

Preface

The Children's Home and Mission and its director, Herbert White, have been names to me since my childhood in Ilford. Cranbrook Road Baptist Church, which I attended, sent its harvest festival goods to what was known as White's Homes which was led by the Orphan Bloke. I later discovered that Herbert disliked the title White's Homes and the "Orphan" was a generic term which covered not only children without parents but also those with one of two parents who could not look after them. One fact was not in doubt, the Home never asked anyone for money and trusted God to meet all its needs. Later, when I was a child care officer working for a local authority, Herbert's successor - Victor White - used to visit our fellowship in Welwyn Garden City. Later still, I became friends with the next White to take over the leadership, Keith White, who recruited me as a trustee of Mill Grove (as it became called).

Herbert White had never sought publicity yet, as I learnt more about Herbert, his colleagues and the Home, I became convinced that here was a story that should be told. Having written previous books, I turned confidently to publishers only to be turned down. The replies were on the lines, "Herbert who? The story of an unknown won't sell." One even suggested that I write about someone famous like Barnardo. Yet it was precisely because Herbert was unknown that I wanted to research and write the book. I am grateful to the Rev. Dennis Paterson of Campaign Literature who immediately and enthusiastically agreed that the biography of Herbert White merited publication and to Ray Brinkley and Marilyn Paterson for so carefully preparing the book.

In the volume, I have attempted two main tasks. First, to re-construct the life of Herbert White and, to a lesser extent, that of his family and colleagues. Second, to try to evaluate the quality of the Home's care within its contemporary context. Much of the material for these purposes has been found within the Home's internal publications. Any quotations which are not specifically footnoted are from reports from the Home's annual meetings or from its magazine *Links*.

In addition, I interviewed or corresponded with a number of people who were workers in or who were children in the Home or who had some other association with it. I particularly wish to thank, Olive Gilbert (nee White), Victor and Margaret White, Keith and Ruth White, Henry Ransome, Minnie Sutton, Joan Warne, Percy Kearns, Bev Savage, Madeline Charlesworth, Robert Tod, Vera Vine, Doris Winter, John Barker, Peggy Chaplin. Some of those interviewed wished to remain anonymous in the text so I have changed the names of all.

Herbert White died over 40 years ago, although the agency he founded still thrives. I believe that his practice, principles and beliefs still have much relevance for today's Christians, for modern social welfare, and for contemporary society.

Bob Holman,
Glasgow,
October, 1993.

Not Like Any Other Home

Contents

I. The Beginnings

Dr Martyn Lloyd-Jones, the leading evangelical figure of his times, declared in Herbert White's presence in 1950,

"I do hope that someone will be able to prevail upon Mr White to write a book not only of his experiences but particularly upon the teaching which he feels is to be derived from what God has done through him."

He went on to compare White with the Christian giants George Muller and Hudson Taylor.

Herbert White never wrote that book. Unlike Muller and Hudson Taylor, books were not written about him. Perhaps the lack explains why this man, whom Lloyd-Jones said he hero-worshipped, should be almost unknown today.

EARLY LIFE

Who was Herbert White? Born in 1878, he was to spend nearly all his life in the London suburb of Woodford. His father was a hard working office worker who provided materially for his wife and 11 children yet was emotionally distant from them. They relied upon a quiet loving mother. Tragically, she died in 1894, crippled by rheumatism, when seven of the children were still under 16. All missed their mother deeply and Herbert later wrote that the impact upon the children "weighed on my mind and I came to the conclusion that there must be some hundreds of boys and girls in like circumstances needing help and guidance." He was only 16 yet the seeds of his life's work were taking root.

Two years later, Herbert obtained a job in a city bank. He had become a Christian in 1891 when another boy led him to faith in Christ and by now he was devoting all his spare time to the Gospel. He assisted at Christian Endeavour and Band of Hope and then became a youthful secretary at the

Baptist Sunday School. He enquired about full-time missionary work abroad but friends were unanimous in advising him to look at the needs around him. Herbert did so and became convinced that God was calling him to help deprived children in Woodford.

Barnardo found Jim Jarvis in the slums of London's East End. Quarrier was horrified to meet children sleeping rough in Glasgow. But today's commuter suburb of Woodford hardly seems the breeding ground of deprived children. However, the Woodford of Victorian Britain was very different from that of today. Much was still rural where farms employed badly paid labourers. The extensive brick-fields, which survived well into the twentieth century, were another source of manual labour. The railway opened in 1856 and thereafter - with easy access to the city - Woodford attracted a growing middle class population. Yet many Victorian middle class householders employed servants who, in or out of work, often found it difficult to cope with their children. It is worth adding that Poor Law records of the time reveal that ex-servants and farm labourers were amongst those most likely to become destitute, partly because, on losing their jobs, they also lost their homes.

Interestingly, two pioneer studies of poverty appeared during Herbert White's formative years. Charles Booth's careful study *Life and Labour of the People of London* was published in 1889. He estimated that 30% of London residents were poor, that is, they had incomes per week of 18-21 shillings to support their families while many had much less and lived in "a state of chronic want."[1] A year later came his namesake William Booth's *In Darkest England and the Way Out.*[2] In it, the founder of the Salvation Army added graphic narratives to Charles's figures. Hunger, illness, homelessness, unemployment, abandoned children, were vividly described. Britain had hordes of poor families and Woodford had its share.

During the twentieth century, conditions certainly improved

in Woodford. In the 1950s, Peter Willmott and Michael Young wanted a more affluent area to contrast with their famous community study of Bethnal Green. They chose Woodford but, somewhat to their surprise, found that 38% of its population were classified as manual workers.[3] Throughout Herbert's lifetime, the affluence of Woodford was to co-exist with some deprivations of the kind that could undermine family life.

ROSA HUTCHIN

At the Sunday School, Herbert explained his vision to another teacher, Rosa Annie Hutchin. To his delight, she shared it. After training in Manchester, Rosa had been rejected by a missionary society on the grounds of her health - she was frail and slightly hunch-backed. She returned to her trade of dress-making and lived in a three roomed flat at 3, the Market, George Lane, Woodford. After prayer together, Herbert and Rosa took the simple yet enormous decision to take in children, with Ma Hutchin (as she was always to be known) providing the day to day care and Herbert looking after the material side. The big day came on November 20th, 1899 when they accepted the nine year old daughter of a lone and drunken father from Barking. The girl, Rosie, arrived frightened and apprehensive. Her fears faded under Ma's love. She was fed, sent to school regularly, taught dress-making, but all these were secondary to the fact that she was cared for by a woman with whom she could talk, confide and trust. The following March another girl was admitted into what was now called a Home for Destitute and Motherless Children.

Events moved rapidly. In April, 1900 the Home moved to a small six roomed house in Latchett Road and, within a year Ma and Herbert were responsible for six girls. One year more and it found its lasting base in Crescent Road. One and then two houses were rented, one for girls, the other for boys. Two workers joined the staff so by April 1903, the Home contained 17 girls and 14 boys. Without any publicity, without any request for money, just enough came for food, furniture, bedding and rent.

Two people called by God to care for deprived children. Then the finding of premises, the taking of more children, the arrival of staff. The foundations of a work which was to endure for nearly half a century were almost in place. Almost but not quite. Two more foundations were to be laid. One was Herbert's marriage, aged 26, to Edith in 1905. Edith was quiet, Herbert was extrovert: she was organised, he was not. Their differences served to unite not divide them. Above all, both were at one that God had called them to work together for children.

The other foundation was Herbert's decision, in November 1906, to leave his secure post at the bank and to concentrate on the Home. He reasoned to himself that if he was preaching faith in God on a Sunday then he should trust God to meet his needs during the rest of the week. Edith fully backed him, as did Rosa Hutchin, but to others his step seemed madness. After all, his salary was used partly to support his wife and their first child Herbert born in 1905, and partly to support the Home. Indeed, it was later revealed that Herbert was contributing £90 a year from his own pocket. Edith's parents were horrified and tried to dissuade him. A local minister called and advised him not to give up certainty for uncertainty. Herbert replied that God was more certain than a bank and he recorded, "The minister left not in a good mood and said he thought I was suffering from a swelled head." Even the bank manager did not want to accept the resignation and exclaimed, "White, you must have gone mad. How are you going to live if you do not receive any money?" Herbert explained that he had already settled that matter with God. The die was cast.

FAITH

What caused Herbert, his wife and Rosa Hutchin to take on such enormous responsibilities with so few material resources? The answer is found again and again in Herbert's own words. On the day they took in the very first child, he said that they were determining to "trust Him alone for all our needs." Five years before he left the bank, the 23 year old White was called in by his bank superiors to explain whether he really was running an orphanage and how could he afford to do it. He told them that he and others were indeed taking in children and that "This work is not a game of chance but is faith in God which is proved by the answers coming." When he did leave the bank in 1906, Herbert wrote, "My greatest reason for so doing is simply an act of obedience to what I believe to be the call of God and the doing away of another prop upon which I had often been tempted to lean, instead of wholly upon Him." The words faith and trust recur throughout Herbert's life and the practice of faith and trust were more central to the Home than the very bricks of the houses. The work had three stated objectives,

> to help needy children:
>
> to be the means of bringing them to know the Lord Jesus Christ as their Saviour:
>
> to trust the Lord alone for all needs without appealing to anyone else.

Herbert and his colleagues believed that the first two objectives would be achieved by the practice of the third, that is trust and faith in a Lord who was both able and willing to provide.

OTHER INFLUENCES

Clearly, Herbert drew his guidance and inspiration primarily from the Bible. What other sources influenced him? Victorian Britain was not without debate on child care issues. As I have shown elsewhere, both the Poor Law and voluntary societies were beginning to explore the value of fostering - boarding-out, as it was called - children with couples. Discussions also raged around the best size for children's homes with some child care agencies introducing what were known as Cottage Homes.[4] These issues seem to have had little impact on the young White. At least he makes little reference to them. However, he did know about the grim conditions in many Poor Law institutions and wanted to prevent children having to enter their portals.

The great child care figure of the time was Dr Thomas Barnardo. Herbert would have known about him. Indeed, there was a Barnardo's in Woodford. In some ways they had similar backgrounds and both were converted in their teens. However, as will be shown later, the kind of homes they developed were to be very different. Further, they displayed a marked contrast in their approaches to raising money. Barnardo was a superb publicist. He made emotional appeals, gave lectures, inserted advertisements, and sold photographs of children. Indeed, as his most recent biographer, Gillian Wagner, says, "He came to regard appealing for funds as part of his ministry."[5] Barnardo thus went directly to the public, Christian or not, and persuaded, even cajoled, them into making donations. He also established his organisation by seeking members of the royal family and aristocracy to identify themselves with it. Herbert was the complete opposite. He refused to make appeals, seek publicity or court the favours of the "great and the good." He was content just to depend upon God.

Herbert had more in common with the Scottish child care giant, William Quarrier. Born in 1829 in Greenock, Quarrier rose from poverty to own a chain of shops in Glasgow. He did not initiate his Orphan Homes in Scotland until he was middle-aged and well known in the Glasgow business community. Herbert, as shown, started his home when still a lowly paid, young clerk. But Herbert would have learnt from Quarrier the necessity for firm confidence in God. Thus Quarrier, looking back at his decision in his fifties, to leave business and to concentrate on the Homes wrote, "He sent all that was required for me and mine in the same way as He did for the Homes."[6] Quarrier's motto was "Have faith in God", the one which Herbert adopted for his work and, indeed, which he wrote over the Home's entrance.

The Christian leader to whom Herbert White makes most reference, however, was neither Barnardo nor Quarrier. It was the Prussian immigrant George Muller who settled in Bristol where he founded a large orphanage. Muller's early and best known biographer, Arthur Pierson, recorded that "His main mission was to teach men that it is safe to trust God's word, to rest implicitly upon whatever He hath said."[7] His trust in God was such that he received £1,500,000 - an enormous sum in Victorian times - without ever asking man for a penny. Muller had published his own autobiography and this, and a number of articles about him, made his work well known to Christians. His death in 1898 was followed the next year by Pierson's biography. Herbert certainly drew upon it. In 1904, he cited approvingly Muller's statement, "God is still the living God, and now, as well as thousands of years ago, He listens to the prayers of His children, and helps those who trust in Him." Herbert looked upon Muller as an example to follow.

By the beginning of this century, Herbert White, with the backing of his wife and Rosa Hutchin, had established a children's home. His motivation, like that of Barnardo, stemmed from Christian compassion and obedience to injunctions in the scriptures to care for the needy. His determination to rely entirely upon God for material support was not a completely new approach in child care and, no doubt, owed something to the examples of Quarrier and

Muller. Interestingly, Herbert was to maintain this faith throughout much of the secular twentieth century. He was to develop a kind of children's home which differed from those of Barnardo, Quarrier and Muller. In the 1990's, Robert Tod, who had been a Home Office inspector in the 1950's, said of the Home, "It was not like any other home at all." Herbert White was to make a significant contribution to the cause of Christianity and to the cause of children.

References

1. C.Booth, *Life and Labour of the people of London,* Macmillan, 1889.
2. W.Booth, *In Darkest England and the Way Out,* Salvation Army, 1890.
3. P.Willmott & Michael Young, *Family and Class in a London Suburb,* Routledge & Kegan Paul, 1960.
4. B.Holman, *Putting Families First,* Macmillan. 1988.
5. G.Wagner, *Barnardo,* Eyre & Spottiswoode, 1979, p.259.
6. A.Gammie, *William Quarrier,* Pickering & Inglis, 1937, p.119.
7. A.Pierson, *George Muller of Bristol,* Pickering & Inglis, 1899, p.364.

II. Prayer Proved 1899-1918

In 1901, the Home for Destitute and Motherless Children issued its first report. It revealed that the number of girls had risen from six to ten. The demands to take more children necessitated more staff - a Miss Grandison was coming - and larger accommodation. The latter was obtained in Crescent Road. Not least, the report stated that all the Home's expenses had been met without advertising the need. From April 1900 to April 1901, it had spent £56-6s-10d, the main costs being rent and rates, food, furniture and clothing. This amount had been forthcoming from donations, from money earned by Ma Hutchin's dressmaking, and from what parents and relatives could afford to pay for their children. The features of this short report were to be reflected and magnified in the following years: the numbers of children continued to climb: more accommodation was sought and found: the multiplying expenses were met by God.

GROWTH

Although the Home never sought publicity, there were always demands upon it to accept needy children. From 1902, it took boys as well as girls so by 1903 it contained 17 girls and 14 boys, a total of 31. A year later it was 40. By 1907, 70 children were crowded in. In 1910, the local Health Authority decided that the Home should not take more than 58 children. Additions to the buildings enabled more to be taken so by the end of the period over 60 children were there. Many of the children spent their entire childhood in the Home, others stayed shorter periods before returning to relatives. Hence every year saw some movement in and out. But whether for short or long stays, the demand to take children was always high.

The growing numbers entailed obtaining more space. And somehow, houses in Crescent Road always became available. By 1906, four houses were being rented and here lived all the children, staff, Herbert, Edith, and their own child, Herbert junior. In 1913, a small house on the other side of the road, "Homecot" was added and the White family moved in. The family now included Olive born in 1909, Ewart in 1910 and soon Eunice joined them in 1914.

THE NEED

Why were so many children in need? The answer lies partly in the social conditions of the time and partly in the shortage of any alternative help. The early years of the twentieth century were ones of prosperity for some, economic distress for others. The bulk of the working population earned under £160 a year. The plight of the 12% of men who were unemployed in 1905 was desperate. Further, lack of adequate food, crowded and unhealthy housing conditions and long-term poverty contributed to a high mortality rate with a third of all men dying before the age of 45. With no unemployment pay, what could the workless do. With no social security benefits what could the widow (or widower) left with the children do? The main recourse was the Poor Law.

The Poor Law was still administered through principles laid down in the Poor Law Amendment Act of 1834. Local parishes elected Guardians who supervised the running of workhouses and limited out-relief. Workhouses would receive only the destitute who had sold all their possessions. Once admitted, inmates were subjected to harsh conditions, wore uniforms, undertook unpleasant tasks like picking oakum or breaking stones, and were usually separated from their children. The latter, as will be shown, were housed in similar degrading institutions. The intention was to stop people from applying. Not far from Woodford was Poplar where, in 1892, another Christian, George Lansbury was elected one of the first working class Guardians. The dread of the workhouse is well illustrated in a letter I found in the Lansbury archives written to Lansbury in 1909 by a Mr Munroe, who earned 6s a week and whose rent amounted to

7s-9d. He states,

> "There is not much left now, and I cannot live on
> the kindness of friends for an indefinite period
> and must soon apply to the Poor Law authorities:
> that is a prospect I view with horror and dread.
> I know it will break my wife's heart to be parted
> from the children, especially the baby boy."[1]

For all the dread, in three months, in the hard winter of
1905, 10,589 persons applied to the Poplar Poor Law.

The only alternative to the Poor Law was charity. As
explained, the nineteenth century witnessed a great rise in
the number of children's voluntary societies. The numbers
they coped with was astonishing with, in 1905, Barnardo's
caring for 11,277 children. Yet many parents disliked
accepting charity and felt that some children's agencies
condemned them as failures and tried to cut them off from
their children.

Thus in the early 1900s, the long-term unemployed and lone
parents, without private incomes or relatives who could
help, faced destitution. A few, it must be said, sought
solace in drink which only made matters worse. Most made
enormous sacrifices for their children until, beaten down,
they took themselves and the children to the Poor Law or
handed the children to a charitable institution. Herbert
White disliked the Poor Law and he understood the reluctance
to seek charity. He determined to run a Home which would
convey neither the condemnation of the Poor Law nor the
stigma of charity. In short, a Christian Home.

The poverty underlying the needs of many families can be
seen in the notes which accompanied children as they entered
the Home. The Home initially gave priority to motherless
children. Herbert's reasoning in 1909 was that "There are
several institutions for fatherless children and entire
orphans" but not the motherless. The policy was almost
certainly allied to Herbert's own loss of his mother and the
impact it had on his brothers and sisters. However, there

is no doubt that children left without a mother and with a father who had to find work were in a vulnerable position. The annual report of 1909 mentions these examples of families who applied to the Home.

* A man, wife dead, earning 23s left with seven children:
* Another widower, with four boys, forced to enter hospital for a serious eye operation:
* Following the loss of his wife, a workman placed his children with a neighbour. This created extra expense yet he could not give up his job.
* Another recent widower left to support nine children on 23s a week.
* A man, trying to establish a business with a fruit barrow, suddenly lost his wife "seven weeks ago". His children, one aged three and a half, were often left alone in the street.

In time, the emphasis on the motherless child lessened. Thus in 1912 Herbert writes of a widow, aged 24 with three children who "has brought the children up very well." She was struggling on parish out-relief, a meagre allowance which some Poor Law Guardians allowed to widows. She could continue in semi-starvation knowing that in the end she and her children would finish up in the workhouse or she could take a post offered to her as a live-in servant and part with the children. She eventually got them a place in the Home where, at least, she knew she could visit them regularly and in the knowledge that if her circumstances changed for the better she could immediately have them back.

So there were motherless children, fatherless children and sometimes parentless children in the Home. In some tragic cases both parents died in quick succession. In others a lone parent could cope no longer and abandoned the children. In 1915, Herbert wrote of such a mother who left her offspring with an elderly woman and never returned. The latter, with an income of 5s a week was paying 2s for her single room. Obviously she could not maintain the youngsters.

The many case notes, which are detailed in the periodic reports circulated by the Home, reveal two major characteristics about the plight of applicants. First, the frequent occurrence of serious illness, injury and death amongst working class families. A father dies when thrown from a cart: another killed in a work accident in a yard: a mother dies young of throat cancer: another suddenly collapses and expires from a stroke: or just the terse comment on a case "mother dead". With no industrial compensation, no national assistance, no rent help, lone parents were placed in an impossible position. If they found employment they could not afford to pay someone to look after the children. If they stayed at home to care then they had no income. Their children were the kind coming to the Home.

Second, the abject poverty which some children had endured even within two-parent families. Children might come from homes freezing cold because parents could not afford fuel. They might walk down Crescent Road without stockings or socks, in rags, even without shoes.

After 1906, the Liberal government did introduce some social reforms which eased the lot of some unemployed and elderly people. But the new insurance payments were set at a low level and applied to only a small part of the population. For destitute people, the main recourse remained the workhouse. Yet the workhouse destroyed families by separating parents from children and making it difficult for them to set up home again. It humiliated them by degrading and harsh treatment. The Home founded by Herbert White and Rosa Hutchin was a Christian response to a cruel society in which the affluent refused to care adequately for the needy. It was a response based on the belief that God, the heavenly father, did not want children to suffer for the wickedness of mankind.

WHAT KIND OF CARE?

Looking back at the Home's early regime and conditions, questions might be raised about its quality of care. Harry Race entered the Home aged eight in 1918. 70 years later he could still remember feeling frightened as he walked up the steps for the first time, then sitting around a little gas stove trying to keep warm with other boys, then going to bed in a dormitory with "bare boards, beds down two sides, sometimes two in a bed." In an interview, he recalled those early days.

> "Every Saturday we had to do a scrub. They taught me to mend shoes so I had to spend my Saturday mornings mending shoes or boots. I became quite efficient and even now I can mend shoes. When I did that I did not have to do other chores like washing-up. We were always hungry, food was pretty meagre for a growing boy. A lot of it was soup and lentils, some meat bones in it to give it flavour. We had two large slices of bread with butter, a mug of cocoa or milky water. We had porridge in the morning, afterwards the burnt was divided out. For tea you had jam on your bread and at night-time you lined up and had a large dose of cod liver oil - with the same spoon. It was a horrible taste but it probably did a lot of good. The place was run on a shoe-string. An apple, an orange, an egg, was a luxury but so it was for other children. We always had a couple of eggs at Easter time. At Christmas we always had a couple of toys as well as an apple and orange. When we went out, someone was always in charge of us, except when we went to school."

Martha Surrey entered the Home in 1908 aged seven. She said,

> "My mother died when she was 37. My father couldn't look after us and the vicar of Walton-on-Thames got us into the Home at Woodford. My

sister also, she was five, nearly six. We were scared stiff to start with.

We had breakfast when we got up, four slices of bread and butter and a drink. Then we went upstairs to the meeting room where we had prayers. The workers walked us to school. I liked school although I was never very brilliant. The teachers treated us all the same but some children called us 'The Homes' kids'. We came home for dinner which was cooked in a great big boiler. It might be lentil soup with dumplings then back to school. Afterwards we played downstairs or chased each other in the garden. Then tea. We never went hungry and at harvest time there were a lot of extras as the churches sent us their harvest. Then prayers taken by Pa White. We slept two in a bed and if it was a single bed, one at the top, one at the bottom.

We were not allowed to play outside the Home but we used to go on outings with the local Sunday Schools. Once or twice we went out to the Rev. and Mrs Barclay's at Hertford Heath for a day in the fields. No motor coaches so we went by horse and waggon.

Ma Hutchin was very good. She had an auntie there as well. We were all a happy crowd. Ma was the one we talked to rather than Pa White but Pa was very sympathetic if you were in any trouble. But you didn't single him out, he singled you out.

When I was a bit older I used to go over the road and look after Mr and Mrs White's children if they went out. There was Herbert, Olive, Ewart, Eunice and Victor. I knew them all as little children. Olive can remember me giving them 'flying angels'. I used to put them on my shoulders and run up and

down the passage. I was baptised at Woodford
Baptist Church when I was 16. Soon after I left
to go into service."

Harry and Martha's accounts reflect those of others. Home
life was characterised by routine, insularity and basic food
levels. Keith White described his grandfather's Home thus,

"Life in the home ran to a smooth, inflexible
routine. At half-past six you got up each
morning, washed yourself and got on with your
appointed job. It might be shoe cleaning, or wood
chopping, or sweeping or potato peeling. After
school each day there were more jobs to do; and
after that a chance to play on the dirt, or to
fish in the river, to try growing plants or even
to rear animals."[2]

Looking back from a 1990's perspective, the Home children
might be judged to have faced hard experiences. Yet
judgement from a 1910's perspective draws forth different
conclusions. Consider working class children who stayed
with their own parents. The 1908 Board of Trade cost of
living survey found that the poorest families were surviving
on 14s-4$\frac{3}{4}$d a week.[3] Their children were constantly
underfed and their meals were neither regular nor
nutritious. Not only were they expected to help in the home
but from an early age were urged to find casual jobs to
bring in a few pennies. They were likely to dwell in over-
crowded and damp rooms, often sharing one bed not just with
brothers and sisters but with their parents. Not
surprisingly, ill-health was the norm rather than the
exception with the children being particularly vulnerable to
death from influenza, measles, diphtheria and tuberculosis.

Obviously, poor children within their own homes did have the
great advantage of the comfort, company and love of their
own parents. In terms of material standards, however, their
lot was no better and, in many cases, far worse than their
counterparts in the Home. Of course, the kind of children

who did enter the Home did not possess stable family backgrounds. It is fairer, therefore, to compare their lot with that of children looked after by the Poor Law - which would have been the residence of many if the Home had not existed.

The Poor Law was a complex organisation. Children might be placed within the workhouses along with adults: in large boarding establishments, often called barrack schools: in smaller family group homes: in foster homes. In 1908 Poor Law children numbered 21,498 in workhouses, 27,698 in residential schools and homes, 8669 in foster homes, and 11,255 elsewhere.

From 1913, it was officially decreed that children aged 3-16 years should not remain in the workhouses yet the practice continued for another 30 years. Their fate was particularly hard in an atmosphere deliberately intended to punish the pauper. They shared wards with the desperately ill, the criminal, the senile. The food was of a low standard because it was supposed to be inferior to what a poor labourer outside could afford. Teaching standards within the workhouse schools were so low that gradually the practice of sending the children to outside elementary schools was adopted. Jack Mitchell recalls local workhouse children who attended his school. He writes, "The boys had closely cropped hair, black jerseys, corduroy trousers, black stockings and heavy boots. The little girls were all dressed alike with their frocks made up of some strong material..."[4] Apart from the crocodile procession to school, the workhouse children were allowed no outside contacts. They had no pocket money, usually no toys or books, not even time to play. Despite the employment of part-time doctors the health conditions inside workhouses were alarming. In 1901, 10.5% of children aged under three, who entered London workhouses, died.

As the century unfolded, more Poor Law children were separated from the workhouses. The barrack schools were large regimes - the 21 units in London housed 17,000 children - run on military lines with frequent corporal punishment, no close relationships with adults, and leisure limited to a supervised walk on Sundays. More fortunate children were in family group homes with perhaps 15-20 children in the charge of one house-mother. These homes were often grouped together in a kind of village. More fortunate, yet the children usually had to undertake all the domestic work and were rarely allowed to mix outside.

Whether in the workhouse, barrack schools or family group homes, Poor Law children endured similar disadvantages. The food was basic, cultural experiences were limited, punishment harsh. True, some exceptional staff, especially house-mothers, did try to bring some comfort and encouragement to their charges. But they were exceptions and the institutionalised children were not compensated by regular contact with their parents. Those in the same workhouse as their mothers and fathers might well see little of them. Those in residential schools and homes might be allowed a monthly visit if within walking distance. If not, contact was difficult to maintain. The result was to weaken family links. Nigel Middleton concludes his study, "Whatever faults were inherent in the Poor Law, and there were many, the consequential destruction of the family must rank as probably the most damaging."[5]

Put against the conditions of contemporary poor children who remained with their parents and, even more, against children in Poor Law institutions, the lot of those in the Home for Motherless and Destitute Children can be seen in a different light. Yes life was routine, children did do domestic tasks, food was basic. But, as Harry Race's wife interrupted him during our interview, at least children like Harry had regular meals unlike poor children like herself who remained with their parents. Yes, living in the Home did bring certain disadvantages but there were compensations when compared with other residential establishments. The domestic tasks were not endless and, once over, the children had leisure time. Harry Race recalls the many games of football on "the dirt", the patch of worn out grass beside the houses. With a tennis ball, sometimes with Herbert joining in, they picked up sides and pretended to be Arsenal, Spurs or West Ham. Harry added, "We were happy. We played football and larked about. We made bonfires and winter warmers." During wet and dark evenings, there were activities inside. Herbert taught them to play chess. There were books and even comics - although Ma disapproved of the latter. A regular feature was a drill club - a popular past-time of the era - in which an instructor from the neighbourhood taught precision marching. The club became so good that it often gave displays outside. From 1912 a musical instructor came and formed a choir which also performed in local churches and clubs. Harry Race was a member and said,

> "Once I slipped into a sweet shop and bought some 'stickjaw' and had to eat it quick. I was in the front row at Leytonstone Baptist Church and I keeled over. The 'stickjaw' made me sick."

The Home children were not allowed to go outside the Home on their own to play. However, sometimes local churches invited them to parties. Before the First World War, the Home did not go on an annual holiday but there were picnics and day outings to places like Epping Forest, Clacton and Southend. Moreover, the children always went to local schools and came home for lunch. Harry Race went to Churchfields School and added, "it was quite a walk and you got the cane if you were late."

The Home children thus had more leisure, more variety, more contact with the neighbourhood than those in Poor Law institutions. Their circumstances were also different in three other ways. First, they were well clothed mainly because Ma was an expert seamstress. The clothes bore some similarities but were not uniforms. Indeed, some outsiders thought them too well dressed and one 1913 correspondent, noting their flannelette vests and shirts, wrote, "If I were a boy I'd say can I come and be one too?" ("one" being a child of the Home). Second, good health, of which more will be said later. Third, contact with relatives. Harry Race said,

"Dad arranged to come and see me once a month and he did and he brought me fruit, sweets and a couple of coppers. He used to give Ma Hutchin something towards my keep. If for the weather or something he never turned up I was very unhappy."

Similarly, Martha Sutton said her father came to see her. Today it is taken as common place child care knowledge that children need to see their parents in order to be reassured that they are loved and loveable. Not so in Victorian and Edwardian times. Thus both Dr Barnardo and the Poor Law held condemnatory attitudes towards parents who could not cope with their children and often classed them as failures who were best kept apart from their off-spring. Herbert White never displayed that attitude. From the third annual report onwards, it was stated that times on Saturday were especially set aside for relatives and friends to visit. Herbert added that these times must "be strictly adhered to unless special permission is obtained." He was not one to have the smooth running of the Home interrupted by unexpected callers. Yet he could be flexible. In 1903, a boy's sixth birthday was due on December 30th and he asked for another Christmas party instead of the usual birthday one. Herbert got his parents and friends to come in and run the party and he recorded, "This was one of the most encouraging events of the year and was greatly appreciated by the children." Unlike many charities whose officials saw their role to rescue children from relatives, Herbert never put barriers in their way. He believed in the family and was pleased when parents could resume their parental position.

The persons best equipped to comment on the quality of care were the children themselves. Few if any recipients of Poor Law care later wrote about it with affection or regarded its staff as their family. On the contrary, Nigel Middleton's study records the dislike, fear, even hatred expressed by inmates such as the young Charlie Chaplin.[6] Yet the annual reports of the Home for Motherless and Destitute Children are full of letters from former children or "old boys and girls", as they were called. To select just a few.

"I am getting on very well indeed. I shall be coming home on the 19th...On Friday I am passing another examination in signals, and if I pass I shall come home with my P.O. boys rating and signal rating. In answer to your last letter I have a Bible and our chaplain gives me a Bible reading card every month and I read my Bible twice a day. Of course, there was a bit of joking, but when they found out I seriously meant to read it they put joking along-side and left me alone." (boy soldier, 1913)

"I was very pleased to receive your letter sometime ago, but you must forgive me for not answering it before. Our battalion has been moved twice since you wrote...... Do you still hear from the old boys. If so, how are they? I am very pleased to know that you pray for me as you will guess there are many temptations in this sphere of life. All that I have been taught in the Home is doing me great service now and I feel as though I cannot thank you enough for all that you did for me." (soldier, 1915)

"...it will not be long before I shall be able to spend a day at Woodford. I have been here a year and eight months, have had three rises, so am now getting £15 a year. Though I like the place and am most comfortable there are times when I wish I was back with you. I feel greatly indebted to the Home for all that you have done for me." (girl in service, 1915)

"I am wondering whether you would come and conduct my wedding service which I am trying to arrange to take place in five months time....as not having been married before I don't quite know how to go about it." (old boy, 1918. Herbert did take the wedding service)

"Just a few lines to let you know that I am still alive and kicking. I have often thought of the different things you told me when I was younger, and my only wish is that I could be with you once again. Lots of things you said would happen, especially when you told me my tongue would lead me into trouble one day. Well it has, on more than one occasion but thanks to God He has preserved me from all danger. I forgot to mention that since I left Woodford I have saved a large amount of money, and of course it's all in the P.O.Bank. I think that was No.1 lesson. Thrift." (officer's steward, 1918)

"At last I can manage to squeeze in time to write you a line, but when one is a mother there is plenty to do.... it is just twelve months today since I saw you, my wedding day...I often look back on the good old times I spent there (at the Homes) and would not mind having them all over again. We hope to come and spend a weekend with you soon as possible." (old girl, 1918)

Of course, these letters may not be representative of all the children. Probably those who did not enjoy their stay would not write. However, it can be said that there were numerous letters. There is no doubt that once the children left the Home, Herbert and Ma tried to keep in touch. They wrote letters, attended weddings, welcomed them back for holidays. Clearly, many former children looked upon the Home as their home and upon its residents as their family. To achieve these bonds of affection for such a large number is a remarkable tribute to the quality of care provided by the devoted staff.

Compared with contemporary institutions, the Home had a liberal approach towards the children, a welcoming attitude towards parents, and a continuing relationship with the old boys and girls. These were unusual features. Herbert White and his colleagues, were pioneers in their progressive child care methods. In time, these features were to be recognised as essential to residential child care in general but the contribution of Herbert and his team has been largely overlooked.

PROVISION

By 1918, the Home had existed for 19 years without any requests being made to humankind for funds. Yet every year up to 60 children had been provided with food, clothes, beds, leisure, affection. How did it happen? The simple but staggering answer is that Herbert, Rosa, and the other members of staff believed God could and would supply their needs. And God did so.

The supplies came not in large cheques from rich patrons, not in huge parcels from wealthy companies. Rather, they came in a multitude of small gifts from ordinary Christians. For instance, in one year the total income of £466-19s-9½d was derived from 758 donations, an average of just 12s per person. Herbert carefully recorded every gift, even to a plate of dripping. Here is his record for two months in 1903.

November
1st.   6s, 16s, 2s.
2nd.   5s
4th.   6s, 1s.
4th.   3s.
7th.   Dripping, bread pudding.
8th.   8s.
10th.   £1-10s, 1s

11th.	£1-1s, 6s, 4s, 6d, £1-5s, 15s.
12th.	Coffee and sugar.
14th.	Pork and apples from Anstey.
15th.	2s, 2s-6d.
18th.	Sack of potatoes, 6s, 10s-6d, 5s.
20th.	12s, 5s, 1s, 1s-6d, £8-7s-10d, being cash taken at sale of work, other amounts paid on other days. 2s.
22nd.	5s, 6s, 2s.
24th.	About 25lbs of sugar.
25th.	Hat and blouse.
30th.	5s-4d, £2.

December

1st.	Dripping, ginger cake, dripping again, 2s.
2nd.	6s, 6s-3d.
3rd.	12s, 8s-6d.
5th.	5s-6d, 11s.
6th.	10s, 2s.
8th.	1s, 12s-7d, 2s-6d.
9th.	6s, 6s, 16s.
10th.	£1.
11th.	Dripping, two loaves, sugar, rice.
12th.	5s.
13th.	3s, 4s, 6s, 4s.
17th.	Some children's clothing, jacket and skirt.
18th.	3s-7d, 4s.
19th.	5s-4d.
20th.	4s, pair of shoes, dripping, dripping again.
22nd.	7s, 6s.
23rd.	2s-3¼d, 3s.
24th.	Cheque for £3-3s, beef, pudding, cake, oranges, nuts, biscuits, in a separate box for each child. This is the second time that the same two friends have provided our Christmas dinner. Toys for Christmas tree, dolls, sweets, fruit, grapes, oranges, apples, dates, cake, cake again, number of little cakes, box of 100 oranges.
25th.	10s, 1s.
26th.	2s-6d.

27th. £2.
30th. 6s.

Here is one month in 1913.
January
1st. 1½lbs of dripping from one of our old girls now in service.
3rd. Alresford 10s, Woodford 14s-1¾d, Leyton £11-3s-7½d being an offering taken at a Bible Class and came as a great blessing. We had been praying the previous midnight especially for God to give us a token today as we were in great need of money and had twelve cases of measles in the Home, thus this came as a special answer to prayer and as a real token from God.
4th. Woodford quantity of parsnips, 16s, 6s-8d, 3s. Readers of Christian Herald £1-5s, Barking 15s, Limehouse 5s, West Ham 12s.
6th. Wingham 2s, one of our old girls 1s-4¾d, another girl 2s.
7th. One hot plum pudding (which came in time for dinner and was greatly enjoyed by the boys).
9th. Isle of Wight £2 and £2-14s.
10th. Southampton 15s, Maidstone 5s, Ilford 19s, Woodford 10s and 10s from a Woodford draper with
"Mrs.....was the successful winner of the competition of guessing how many handkerchiefs in a model of the Woodford Memorial Hall we exhibited in our window and has selected your home to receive the prize."
Woodford 6s-8d, 3s.
13th. Egypt £10 with
"Thanks for your letter also for the LINKS received from time to time. I was very sorry to hear of the outbreak of measles and hope by this time you are over the worst of it."
Limehouse 5s, Deal 5s with
"Just a little thank offering from your box for your family. May the Lord abundantly

bless you and make you a blessing. HE NEVER FAILS THOSE WHO PUT THEIR TRUST IN HIM, affectionately yours in the Risen Lord."

15th.   Quantity of parsnips, Wandsworth £1.

16th.   Anon 6 rabbits, 1 parcel of second hand clothes and boots from Westcliff, 1 parcel containing 9 flannelette petticoats, 1 cotton petticoat, 1 bonnet, 4 pairs knickers, 3 woollen vests from a Church mission in Walthamstow.

17th.   From Chingford Hatch 1 pinafore, 1 pair of pants, 1 petticoat, 6 scrap books, some texts etc.

18th.   Isle of Wight 19s-6d, Highams Park £1, Camden Town 10s, Hampstead 12s, Limehouse 5s.

20th.   2lb fish.

23rd.   Anstey 10s.

24th.   Woodford 5s 1d with
"I enclose postal order being a contribution from the scholars of our Mission Sunday School towards your funds."
Chelsea 8s, Ireland 10s.

25th.   Barking 15s.

27th.   Goodmays, second hand sewing machine with 2s-6d to cover expenses of putting same in order and 4 yards black serge. Limehouse 5s, Brentwood 5s, Woodford 13s-4d, 12s-6d.

28th.   Woodford 5s.

30th.   Tunbridge Wells 2s-6d, Woodford 10s, Sevenoaks £3.

31st.   Alresford 10s.

The Home's existence was thus a hand to mouth one. Every day the staff had to rely upon God. Every day He provided. But sometimes it was a close call as these further extracts reveal.

May 10th, 1902.   Funds had sunk very low and we were placed in great need for the day's provisions. Having told the Lord we were looking to Him, we found 6s put through the letter box in an envelope without any sign as to who from, and after more prayer friends called and left 10s, 1s-9d, 7s-6d.

May 12, 1902.   Being over-run with mice we asked the Lord to send two cats along, one for each house, which He did in less than two days.

Sept.1st, 1902.   Had come to the end of our store so unitedly asked the Lord for more, and scarce had we risen from our knees when 10s was left, and a little later 1s-4$\frac{1}{2}$d and some apples, which set us off singing. I believe God answers prayers - I have proved God answers prayer, glory to His Name.

Jan.9th, 1903.   We have been marvellously delivered today. Last night the funds were all exhausted and £2 required to make up rent for which the Lord directed me specially to pray. Nothing came by the first post, but by six o'clock in the evening £3-7s had come in, thus the Lord gave us more than we asked or thought.

May 30th, 1913.   From Woodford 6$\frac{1}{2}$lbs of mutton arrived whilst we were praying for our dinner and just came in good time.

One summer, the children were looking forward to the annual excursion, with other local Sunday Schools, to Clacton. A week before, the money was not available. By the appointed day, not only had sufficient cash come in but enough to give the children some spending money.

At the Home's Annual Meeting in 1915, Herbert dwelt on the theme of God's answers. He said,

"I want to tell you some of the answers to prayer which we have had. We were praying a short time ago one Saturday morning, that God would send us funds to carry us over the week-end, and about a quarter of an hour after we had risen from our knees, we heard a knock at the door, and when we went we found it was a telegraph boy with a telegram. And I said to my wife, "What's the matter now?" You see, I hadn't sufficient faith. Something was the matter, but very different from what I expected. When we opened the telegram we found that someone who lived 65 miles away from where we were praying had wired £5 for the Woodford work, for which we praise God. (Applause). Then, last Easter, we had been able to pay the King's Taxes but we hadn't anything with which to pay our quarter's rent. I had to go away in the country and when I left home I hadn't a penny piece towards the rent. But when I got to the place, a friend came up to me and said, "Glad to see you down here again. Here's a pound for your work." Then a young lady came to me and said, "Here's 8s 6d. for the Home," and in the evening a friend gave me a cheque for thirty shillings in the name of the Lord. Another friend came up before the meeting was over and said, "Put this in your pocket and don't open it until you get back." When I did open it I found it was £25 in the name of the Lord. (Applause). We woke up this morning, and just to keep us from being pessimistic, by the first post there came from a friend many miles from here, £25 in the name of the Lord."

Each year, the Home's expenditure rose but, almost in exact proportion, so did income. For the year April, 1900 to April, 1901, the Home's income was £54-15s-2$\frac{3}{4}$d. By 1905 it was £332-13s-11$\frac{1}{2}$d which met all costs with a balance of 11$\frac{3}{4}$d. By 1913 to 1914, income was £654-6s-3$\frac{3}{4}$d. The outbreak of war in 1914 put up costs as inflation hit the very goods, particularly food and milk, which 60 children required. With citizens having to spend more on themselves and with a growing number of male wage earners drafted abroad in the armed forces, it might have been expected that at last the Home would carry a deficit. But that is to underestimate both God and the faith of the staff. Receipts for the year ending April, 1917 were up to a record £747-17s-6½d which left a balance of £6-17s-2½d once all costs had been met.

It should be added that the Whites did not accept money given to the Home for their own personal support. They knew that a God who could meet the needs of the children could meet the needs of His servants. In 1909, Herbert wrote,

> "It does not seem to be generally known that no salaries are paid to any of the workers who simply receive their board and lodgings and whatever the Lord may specially send for that purpose. We have no props whatsoever on which to lean, no grant or annuity, no special church to whom we can look for help but solely upon the arm of God."

He continued that he and the other staff had been given holidays and added, "We have also received at sundry times clothes which have greatly helped us, personally I have not bought any clothes for over four years. I should also like to mention the fact that the extra expense incurred by the arrival of my little daughter in January last was met by a kind friend, which was in direct answer to prayer and greatly relieved us." Two years later, Herbert rejoiced that God had provided holidays for Ma Hutchin, his wife and children at Westcliff while he spent the fortnight in a Gospel Car spreading the Good News throughout Kent. Typical Herbert. In 1912, he was recording that not only had a friend paid for him to attend a conference but another "stopped me and asked me if I would accept a new silk hat."

The Lord exceeded all of Herbert's expectations - and more. In 1903, he stated that at times "there has been the thought of appealing to those we know for assistance" but he never did and he and his colleagues continued to depend upon God's promise to undertake for them. For a few years, the Home drew in income from an annual Sale of Work. In 1905 this was abandoned and replaced by two days of prayer praise and thanksgiving, an event which was to become known as "Our Day". In 1902, Herbert gave up his intention to buy the first house "as I felt that the Lord would not hold with our being in debt, and arrangements have been made to rent both the houses, with power to buy either or both should the Lord answer our daily prayer and send us the means so to do, and only those funds shall be applied for this purpose which are expressly given for it." However, at times, it seemed as though not even the rent would be paid. On one occasion, Herbert was still praying for the rent when the landlord called. Before asking for his dues, the landlord handed over a collecting box in which his father had been putting aside money for the Home. The contents plus what Herbert already had totalled exactly the quarterly rent. As Keith White put it, "The landlord had brought his own rent."[7]

PEOPLE

The good Lord supplied more than food, clothes and money. He sent people. The Home never advertised for staff for the faith principle applied here as in everything else. In 1901, a Miss Grandison joined and was followed by her friend Mrs Wilson who not only sold her home in Perth but also gave liberally to the Home. It was Mrs Wilson's appointment which enabled the doors to be opened to boys as well as girls. By 1903, Miss Grandison had been replaced by a Mrs Mary Dyer while, at the same time, an aunt of Ma Hutchin - a Miss F. Hutchin - also came. By 1908 both Mrs Wilson and Mrs Dyer had left. A Miss O. Hall joined and when she departed, probably in 1911, the Home was short of helpers. The need was promptly laid before God and Herbert wrote in 1912,

> "We had also been praying for some time past that God will touch the heart of one of His children to come as a helper into the work and today our friend Miss L Lawrence has been led to join us for which we praise God."

No doubt, looking after 60 children was demanding work and

soon Herbert was requesting prayer that Miss Lawrence's "nerves may be strengthened." She endured until 1913. A pattern can be seen. Herbert, his wife Edith, and Ma stayed permanently: those like Miss F. Hutchin proved stable staff members over several years: others came for two to three years: and, it appears, local friends from the vicinity came in to help when necessary.

Herbert may have been the inspiration of the Home. Edith was his constant support. Yet there can be little doubt that Ma Hutchin was the lynch-pin of the day-to-day caring and organisation. Her small frame carried a dignity and calm which influenced the whole establishment. From early morning she oversaw the preparation of meals, the cleaning, the getting ready for school. She found time to mend clothes and, in the early days, to make some as a source of income. And, in the evenings, she would gather a few children around her to read and tell them stories.

Unlike Herbert, Ma did not write a diary or frequently address public meetings. Hence it is more difficult to build up a picture of her. But former children always spoke warmly of her. For instance, in 1912 a former girl wrote to recall an incident when she was ten,

> "We had just finished breakfast, and on leaving the table Miss Hutchin - who we called mother, and she was indeed a mother to us, came into the dinning room and said, 'I want you to go to the Post Office and change this postal order' - it was the first I had ever changed."

Two things were important to the girl. One was that Ma trusted her with the money. The other was that, on her return, Ma praised her for being so quick.

Sometimes Ma did say a few words at the annual meetings. At one she thanked the friends who had brought material so that she could make clothes for the children. She added, "We have new things to put on the children....Only mothers of large families know what it means to have a new garment ready for a child whenever it wants one." At another meeting, she urged parents, "never tell a child that if it was a naughty boy or a naughty girl, they would send it to a Home." She explained that this created an impression of a Home as something bad and nasty whereas in reality theirs was "a Home of love." In an era when children in institutions were often told that they were lucky to be treated even as second class citizens, Ma's attitude is a remarkable one. She wanted the very best for the Home's children. Such an aspiration was not to become widespread for another 30 years.

Ma was concerned about more than material well-being. In 1914, she said,

> "Our temporal need is great, but our spiritual
> need is greater. It is souls we are after, though
> we are clothing the bodies. It is our aim and our
> work that souls may be won for the Master."

Ma had wanted to be a missionary. God diverted her to the task of caring for the physical and spiritual needs of children in Britain. It was a task for which she was superbly fitted.

God also provided the Home with an enriching band of helpers and friends. Some who came in to cook, to paint, to garden, are now nameless. Others are recorded. Most mentioned is Dr Martin Flegg. In 1901, Herbert visited a local church warden who was also a doctor. On hearing of the Home, Dr Flegg asked to see it. During his visit, the doctor asked where the money came from and Herbert told him of their reliance upon God. A few days later, he returned and offered to be the Home's doctor. He then fulfilled this role for 33 years without ever charging for his service. In those pre-NHS days, medicine was expensive with regular care restricted to the privileged few. Yet God gave the Home a skilful doctor, who called regularly to check the children and who was on call at any time. The quality of his interest and ability was soon evidenced in May, 1902 when a girl fell dangerously ill after eating poisonous leaves from a hedge. Dr Flegg called constantly, three times in one day, to ensure that she pulled through. Of course, children did die. In 1906 the killer illness diphtheria broke out. Dr Flegg's faithful ministering and the hiring of two fully qualified nurses limited the deaths to two. In 1912-13, measles raged yet, remarkably, no children died in the Home. During these years, diphtheria, measles and influenza epidemics swept through Britain claiming many young victims. Death rates were particularly high in Poor Law institutions. The health record of the Home was thus astonishingly good. The doctor modestly attributed this to the sound diet and loving care provided by the staff. In truth, much if not most credit must go to him. Not only did he keep at bay the epidemics, he also sought specialist treatment for children with disabilities. Thus in 1914, a stay at the Felixstowe Convalescent Home was arranged for a boy suffering from acute rheumatism. Another, who had lost the use of his right leg following a stroke, was enabled to have an operation and the fitting of a surgical boot. The health care of the Home's children was thus far better than for the majority of children in Britain.

Dr Flegg was tall and dignified. He invariably wore spats and did his round in a horse drawn trap. In presenting his medical reports at the annual meetings, he spoke briefly and wryly. Yet clearly he had a warmth and concern which radiated to children. Harry Race, who at the age of 13 worked as a delivery boy for him, simply described him as "a wonderful man." Flegg, like Herbert White, diverted such praise from himself to his God.

An accountant, Albert Willmott, rendered service as honorary auditor for many years. From 1907, a Mr Watson began a long association as the Home's dentist. Apart from these professionals, other Christian folk began to identify what they could do. On January 6th, 1906, eight women met at 104, Lansdowne Road, Seven Kings and began making clothes for the children. In their first year, they made pinafores, nightdresses, overalls and underclothes, 185 items in all.

By 1910 it was 278 garments. Other sewing meetings were formed making seven by 1916. In June, 1909, three friends formed a boot club which collected weekly pennies from supporters and which allowed 43 pairs of boots to be purchased in one year. Soon after, another boot club was added. These groups thus ensured a steady flow of new clothes and new boots so saving much expense for the Home.

As the number of friends increased - without any publicity - so the staff decided on an annual meeting both to report progress to the friends and also to praise God. The programme for these meetings was long by today's standards. For instance, the 13th annual gathering, held in a large tent in May 1912, had meetings at 3.30pm and 7.30pm. The afternoon one of two hours duration consisted of two hymns, prayer, singing by the children, two solos and addresses by the Rev. Thornton Duxberry, Ma Hutchin, Mr George Goodman and Mrs Florence Barclay. The evening format was similar plus a short report by Dr Flegg and a longer one by Herbert.

Mrs Barclay was a regular speaker since 1905. Clearly the children enjoyed her talks and, after one meeting, Herbert noted that "she spoke with that quiet, magnetic power, which always characterises her oratory." Florence Barclay was more than a speaker. She was a famous novelist. Born in 1862, the daughter of a vicar, she married the Rev. Charles Barclay in 1881. She was a woman of remarkable energy, masses of dark hair, and a rich contralto voice. She was a fine sportswoman who played golf, captained a women's cricket team and once cycled the 120 miles from Hertford Heath to Cromer in one day. She bore eight children yet still had time to travel abroad, address meetings and support charities. In 1908 she published the first of 11 novels. Her second, in 1909, *The Rosary*, succeeded immediately and sold over a million copies. *The Mistress of Shenstone*, 1910 was later made into a film. In 1912, Florence suffered a cerebral haemorrhage following an accidental blow to the head and her writing career seemed over. Astonishingly, soon after she was cured by another blow from an oar while boating at Keswick. Other books followed. *The Following of the Star* is typical Barclay, a romantic, even sentimental tale, which was sneered at by some intellectuals but which far outsold their books. It tells of a young missionary on furlough who is attracted to a beautiful woman due to inherit a fortune providing she marries within a short time. She proposes to the missionary. The book is well crafted, the characters cleverly portrayed, and each chapter ends with the reader wanting to know what comes next. Mrs Barclay even makes some muted points about society's oppression of women and it is of interest that she became president of the East Herts Women Voters' Association. Her interest in the Home was no passing fad. She kept in regular contact and often presented all the children with a book, picture or other gift. In 1915, when the war prevented the usual trip to the seaside, she had them all to her home at Hertford Heath. Her biographer notes "The charitable work in which she took the greatest personal interest was the Home for Motherless Children at Woodford."[8] Houses, food, money, clothes, friends, staff, even a nearby location for an outing, God provided them all. No wonder Herbert was continually praising God.

A CHRISTIAN HOME

Clearly, two of the three objectives were being met, "to help needy children" and "to trust the Lord alone for all needs." What of the third. to bring them "to know the Lord Jesus Christ as their Saviour"? There could be no doubt that this was a Christian Home. Herbert led prayers, choruses and a little talk every day. Sunday might mean attending three meetings. The Home eventually had its own Sunday School with teachers coming in from the surrounding area. In 1912, the annual report recorded that the Sunday School had been saving money to support a young man in India training to be an evangelist. The children often memorized scriptures for which they were awarded certificates. This emphasis on religion was not unusual in these times. The Poor Law establishments had their own part-time chaplains. At nearby Dr Barnardo's Village Home, G.V.Holmes recalled that everyday started with worship and that on Sundays even play was around Bible themes and that children were expected to be prepared for confirmation.[9] Religion could be a cold, formal, routine. Nigel Middleton complains that it was sometimes applied to children "as a soporific to keep them complacent, not as a constructive doctrine which might lead to personal philosophy and way of life."[10] This accusation could not be levelled at the Home for Destitute and Motherless children for the staff and atmosphere were distinctly unsoporific. Mrs Edith White conveyed calm yet positive trust in God, Ma Hutchin conveyed the compassion of Christ, and Herbert White radiated the power of the Holy Spirit. In a Home where dinner sometimes depended on the prayers at breakfast, Christianity had to come over as a dynamic force.

Herbert and his colleagues believed that children could and should be converted to the Lord. They were delighted when youngsters made personal decisions. Of course, some did not respond. Harry Race tells of a friend in the Home who, in later life, "wasn't religious. He reacted against what he had been taught." Others, like Harry, while not fully committing themselves as children, appreciated the Christian atmosphere and ethos. He said,

> "It's been with me all my life. When I came back
> from Canada and couldn't get work, I wouldn't
> steal."

Many did respond as children and took their faith with them when they left the Home. Many letters give evidence of the Christian faith of the old children. Particularly touching is one sent to Ma in 1912. A boy wrote,

> "I often have to pray for strength to overcome my
> temper, but Jesus is always ready to help me. I
> do so miss you dear mother. If only I could talk
> to you as we did at home...We know that all things
> work together for good to them that love God.

Romans 8:28."

In yet others, seeds were sown which took root and grew years later. Harry Race's own faith flourished in later life and he recalled going to Australia and there meeting "a former White's boy who went to Australia 26 years ago, was converted seven years ago, gave up his job as a builder and now helps in a Children for Christ organisation."

THE GREAT WAR

Historical and political events seemed to have made no great impact on Herbert. The death of Queen Victoria, the coronation of the new king, the great social reforms of the Liberal government, are not mentioned in surviving records of his sermons and reports. Even the Great War is not commented upon in the April and May, 1914 editions of *Links,* as the Home's newsletter became called. Yet the war soon forced its attention upon the Home. Olive White, born in 1909, recalls sheltering in the basement from the air raids of, probably, 1915, and singing choruses to maintain their spirits. Paper became hard to obtain and *Links* shrank in size. Food prices rose sharply as shortages intensified but the children never went without. Meanwhile, they responded by knitting mittens for soldiers and completed 100 pairs by March, 1915.

The most marked effect of the war was in the recruitment of former Homes children into the armed forces. By 1916, 21 were in the army or navy, three of whom had been wounded and one of whom was a prisoner of war in Germany. Dr Flegg and Mr Watson had volunteered with the former active in the front in France. Then on October 17th, 1917 Bertram McGahey was killed in action in Egypt. Bertram had come to the Home, with his sister, when he was seven. He spent his last leave at the Home and, following it, wrote to Herbert,

"I should like to thank you for your kindness to me in allowing me to come and stay with the old friends. I can truly say it is the only place I can call HOME and it has been a good home to all

the children who have passed through it, and also
to myself."

Herbert's heart must have been full as he penned Bertram's
obituary. At least he could devote himself to the 60
children still in the Home. Yet suddenly the war threatened
to remove him. Conscription was introduced and, although in
his thirties, Herbert was eligible. His appeal to a
tribunal for exemption was rejected. Herbert, Edith, Ma and
the others appealed against the decision and committed the
matter to prayer. Fifty ministers of religion supported his
appeal. The Appeal Tribunal then exempted Herbert on the
grounds of his poor feet - he did always suffer from bunions
- but required him to work in a munitions factory in East
London. So for much of the war, Herbert had to leave
Crescent Road at 6am, do a long day's toil and then return
to attend to the Home - not forgetting his own wife and
children. But the God who answered the prayers for
exemption also heard those for extra strength for him to
continue. Then came peace. Herbert could look back on 19
years in which the Home had cared for 250 children. In
December, 1918, he wrote,

> "We are able with hearts full of praise to declare
> that in answer to prayer He has brought us
> through. We have been and are free from sickness
> and debt and we want to acknowledge that 'He did
> it'."

The Children in 1906

The Home in 1906

Ma Hutchin, an early photograph

Dr Martin Flegg

Children and Staff in 1910. Herbert White is in the middle of the second row from the bottom, with his wife Edith on his right and Ma and Fanny Hutchin on his left

Herbert White talking with soldiers during the First World War

References

1. B.Holman, *Good Old George: the Life of George Lansbury,* Lion, 1990, p.59.
2. K.White, *A Place for Us,* Mill Grove, 1976. pp.29-30.
3. N.Middleton, *When Family Failed,* Gollancz, 1971, p.53.
4. E.J.Mitchell, *A Cornishman Remembers,* Campaign Literature, 1991, p.10.
5. N.Middleton, *op.cit.,* p.309.
6. N.Middleton, *op.cit.,* pp. 98-99,175.
7. K.White, *op.cit.,* p.24.
8. *The Life of Florence Barclay,* by one of her daughters, Putnam, re-printed 1930, p.224.
9. G.V.Holmes, *The Likes of Us,* Frederick Muller Ltd., 1948.
10. N.Middleton, *op.cit.,* p.310.

III. Between The Wars 1919 - 1939

Post-war Britain seemed a land of hope with a government elected on a manifesto to build a society "fit for heroes". Certainly, the inter-war years did witness some developments in welfare provision. In 1918, local education authorities were given the duty to ensure medical treatment for school children although, outside of school, medical help remained beyond many families. Schools also initially expanded the distribution of milk and meals. Many local authorities also took advantage of permission to build council dwellings so that, in 1939, 121,658 were constructed. Further, in 1929, responsibility for the Poor Law passed from parishes to the better equipped Public Assistance Committees of local authorities.

Even more significantly, central government was accepting more responsibility for the relief of poverty. The new Ministry of Pensions awarded incomes to families who had lost their main wage earner in the war. Noticeably, officers' children received far bigger grants than those of other ranks. In 1920 the national insurance scheme was extended to cover more workers. However the cover still helped only selected trades for a short period of unemployment, while women workers were excluded altogether. In 1934 the creation of the Unemployment Assistance Board was an indication that the government recognised the seriousness of the plight of those without work.

The legislation was gradual and episodic. Its limitations were revealed as the economic crisis deepened. As early as 1921 the warning signs were apparent in Glasgow where the council had to install soup kitchens for the poor while private landlords evicted 2,000 families for non-payment of rent. Prices and wages continued to fall. In 1930, unemployment reached two and three quarter million and thereafter touched three million. The government responded by cutting expenditure. Some education authorities had to abolish school meals just when they were most needed. National insurance payments were cut by ten per cent. The National Assistance Board imposed stringent means tests which were much resented. With no other forms of income, many families had to turn again to the Poor Law and the workhouse. In any one day in the 1930s, about one million people were being assisted by the Poor Law. Thus George Lansbury, the Christian Socialist leader of the Labour Party, who had spent a lifetime battling against the workhouse, had to write in 1934 that they were still looking for a time when, "we shall not be cursed by the penal poor law, and nobody, not even the worst among us, will be left to starve."[1]

Victims of the continuing poverty were children. William Beveridge, in his famous book *Full Employment in a Free Society*, stated, "Nearly half of all persons discovered in Want by the social surveys of British cities between the wars were children under 15. Nearly half of all working class children were born into Want."[2]

That so many children survived at all, owed much to the careful budgeting on low wages or dole money and the self-sacrifice of parents. But a price had to be paid and Middleton points to research showing it was often paid by the ill-health or even death of mothers.[3] The combination of poverty and bad health thus continued to be behind the break-up of many families. The Woodford Home was therefore still receiving children for the same reasons as before the war as the following cases illustrate.

Two boys entered the Home after their widowed mother suffered terminal cancer.(1921)
Two girls and a boy received after their lone mother died.(1921)
Two girls and two boys whose mother was in a sanatorium and father in bad health taken in.(1921)

A child accepted as mother in a mental hospital and father out of work.(1929)

Another child taken because the father was dead and "mother in delicate health and has since been in hospital undergoing an operation."(1929)

Children received because "Father dead, mother left with three under seven years, she struggled on working for them but her health broke down and doctor says she must part with the children."(1929)

A man returned from America where his wife had died: he could not find work and did not qualify for the dole: a church enabled him to eat with a small allowance from its Communion Fund while his child was taken by the Home.(1933)

A letter from a mother to the Home stated, "I am suffering from cancer and as my little girl on my death would be left to the mercy of the world - as I have no near relatives - I am hoping you will find it possible to take her into your orphanage." Two weeks after the child entered the Home, the mother died.(1933)

An unemployed and widowed man in "squalid surroundings", brought his 8 year old daughter to the Home.(1933)

A 71 year old man lost his younger wife: he had to seek admission to a Home for Old Men and his 10 year old boy was accepted into the Home: sadly, six months later, just after visiting his son, the father was killed in a road accident.(1934)

Another widowed man paid an elderly lady to look after his two children while he worked: on her death, he had to give up work but found himself without money: the Home took the children.(1934)

EXPANSION NOT STAGNATION

Social historians do not regard the inter-war years as notable ones in the care of deprived children. Within the Poor Law, some improvements did occur with attempts made to reduce the size of institutions. A few individuals did make remarkable achievements. In Poplar, George Lansbury, on becoming chairperson of the Poor Law residential school,

abolished the seven course dinners served by children to
managers, appointed capable staff and introduced sport and
vocational training. The school was moved out to Shenfield
where it became regarded as a model school.[4] But this was
exceptional. Generally, Poor Law institutions remained
regimented and dull. Thus Middleton points to several
official reports "which showed that in the Poor Law
institutions the general care of children was of a poor
standard."[5] He shows that as late as the 1930s, some
workhouses contained wire netting which divided children
from fathers and through which they kissed. No wonder
parents still regarded the Poor Law as the last resort.

The many voluntary societies continued to accommodate many
children, including 15,000 placed with them by the Poor Law.
Yet, in terms of developing new methods, they had stagnated.
The Waifs and Strays Society (later the Church of England
Children's Society) had been a go-ahead agency which
pioneered small residential homes and fostering in Victorian
times and which won much financial support especially from
Anglicans. Yet, as its historian John Stroud reveals, by
the 1920s and 30s it was running out of ideas and money. He
wrote, "By 1931 it was clear that the General Fund - which
had always been the backbone supporting the whole body of
the Society's activities - was running an accumulating
deficit...There was a clear crisis of confidence."[6]
Retrenchment had to be imposed and new schemes abandoned.
Another example is found in the moving autobiography of
Dorothy Haynes who wrote in appreciation of the time she
spent at the famous Aberlour Orphanage from 1929 to 1933.
The orphanage contained devoted staff but its isolated,
austere, even spartan, care of 500 children was little
different from that given in Victorian times.[7] Noticeably,
Professor Thomas Fergusson, in his historical background to
Scottish child care, goes from 1914 to 1946 with no mention
of any notable progress.[8] Overall, the child care
voluntary societies were no longer in the leading positions
which had been achieved by the likes of Barnardo, Rudolf and
Stephenson. Stagnation had set in.

The same could not be said for the Home for Destitute and Motherless Children. Stagnation and Herbert White just did not go together. The Home was under pressure from two sources. An outside pressure stemmed from the growing economic depression which resulted in large numbers of children needing care. An internal pressure arose from staff members' desire to improve facilities and standards for the children. The outcome was continual expansion both in numbers and living conditions in the very period when most agencies were concentrating on survival and cut-backs.

The will of Private Bertram McGahey divided his money between his sister, herself an old girl from the Home, and the Home itself. The latter amount £8-18s-9d became a seed in Herbert's fertile mind as he pondered how to use it in a way which would also preserve Bertram's memory. The four houses were crowded and lacked playing facilities, particularly in wet weather. Initially, Herbert thought of constructing a wooden hut but he soon realised this would not be sufficient. Further, he was becoming convinced that the neighbourhood needed a building for Christian meetings. After prayer with his colleagues, he erected a sign on "the dirt" which said, "Site for new hall." The estimate for a two-storey building was up to £5,820. Bertram's money along with another initial contribution amounted to £112. At the time, the total annual income of the Home was only £1,300. Further, Herbert would not contemplate a mortgage or any kind of debt. It seemed impossible. Impossible to humankind but not to God. Herbert instructed the builders to start. Moreover, he insisted on materials of the highest quality with the floors made fire resistant. Only the best was good enough for the children. Slowly the building went up and gradually the money came in. The seven staff who looked after the children daily each contributed £1 from their tiny incomes for a new gas stove. By 1928 it was complete. Florence Barclay had died in 1921 and the building was named the Florence Barclay Memorial Hall. Opened on July 5th, 1928, by Mrs Barclay's youngest daughter, Mrs Angela Whitcombe, it consisted of a top floor made up of a large hall, ideal for games, and a stage with downstairs a dinning room, wash basins, kitchen and lockers for all the children. The overall cost was £2,250 and, at the opening, £1,400 had been paid. What of the remaining £850? Had faith failed? No, the agreement stated that this had to be paid within six months of completion. And it was. As Herbert said at the opening,

"There is a bigger power in prayer than we dream of. There is nothing that God cannot do if we trust Him. We have learned this secret that one person with God is in the majority."

In the same year, Herbert, ever keeping with the times, changed the old fashioned name Home for Destitute and Motherless Children to the Children's Home and Mission. This Home now had a well equipped hall and was not a penny in debt.

The Children's Home and Mission owned a hall where the children could play and eat but it did not own the four houses where they slept. Yet, as Herbert revealed, for years, "we have been praying that God would move the heart of someone to purchase the property for us." In 1930, Dr Frederick Marsh, a local and godly minister, informed Herbert that he wished to do just that. The landlord, having received rent for over 20 years, generously agreed to sell the four houses for £1,700. To put the icing on the cake, another Christian agreed to re-decorate them free of charge. Thus on January 3rd, 1931, Mrs Ethel Marsh unveiled a plaque to commemorate the handover. Dr. Marsh then dedicated the houses to the memory of five of their nine children who had died. Six weeks later, Dr. Marsh himself died. For nearly 30 years the Home had owned no property. Now it possessed four houses and a hall. Before 1931 was out, two more house in Crescent Road had been presented. They had fallen vacant and the Stark family - long time supporters - purchased and presented them in memory of their father who had recently died. All this happened without the staff asking anyone but God and all in the years when Britain was experiencing a great economic depression. The

Rev. Louis Parkinson, pastor of the local Baptist Church had watched the Home grow and said in an address at the annual thanksgiving.

"When Mr White was speaking I could not help thinking of the time when he and Miss Hutchin started the work with one child. I wonder what they would have said then if anyone had come to them and told them that thirty-one years hence they would be feeding eighty-three children and that they would possess a block of premises which would be the envy of many people. I think they would have said it was a dream."

The accumulation of property prompted Herbert, and perhaps others, to consider the legal standing of the Home. It was a private venture in which money was paid directly to Herbert. It ran smoothly because he was a man of integrity plus administrative acumen. But what if he died? Who would own the property and appoint his successor? On 31st December 1930, a trust was established. The deed was signed by 13 members including Herbert, Edith, Ma Hutchin, Mrs Ethel Marsh, James Stark and eight others. It re-stated the three objectives of the work, namely

to receive destitute or needy children:

to bring children to know the Lord Jesus Christ as their Saviour:

to prove that God is able to answer prayer by appealing to Him alone for workers, funds etc.

The deed established that the property and resources of the Home belonged to the trustees. However, it is noticeable that, during his lifetime, considerable powers still rested with Herbert who, as founder and director, appointed staff and trustees. Nonetheless, the Home was now on a sound legal footing and registered with the Charity Commissioners.

Before long, the trustees became responsible for yet more property. As the Home became more crowded and as Woodford became more urbanised, so Herbert longed for a holiday and convalescent centre in the country. The vision and prayer was shared with the trustees and eventually just the place came on the market. The Grove in Tiptree was a Georgian, double fronted house set in seven acres and priced at £1,250. Four friends came forward with the money while other gifts provided a further £840 for alterations and equipment. Still more was added when three supporters purchased an adjoining area of nearly two acres ideal for growing vegetables. The Grove was officially opened on July 16th, 1938 with a praise meeting attended by nearly 400 people, including the children. The latter stayed for the whole of August and in Herbert's words, "had a right royal time, playing in the fields, trying to catch fish in the lake etc. A friend sent us along a see-saw which greatly delighted the children, and to make a break we had two outings to Maldon...We feel this was all worth while, as over 60 returned built up by the holiday and ready for winter. Hallelujah!"

Staff, money, hall, houses, holiday centre. During the inter-war years, the Lord provided the facilities which enabled the Home both to take more children and to improve standards of care. Not stagnation but expansion.

THE CHILD'S VIEW

The houses, the hall, the holiday centre were essential but they do not make up the Home. The buildings in Woodford still stand today but they do not convey what it was like to be there in those years. For this, it is best to listen to those who were there as children.

James Barnes, now in his 70's, wrote to me, "It was in 1932 that I was sent to the Home where there were 60-70 children. I was an orphan in the true sense of the word and, as a child, knew no other home. Indeed, until the war, when I joined the R.A.F., I knew no other parents than Mr & Mrs White.

Mr Herbert White was a patriarchal figure, very fair and very strict. Life in the Home was spartan - for all of us there. It must have been very arduous for him dealing with the lives of the unfortunate.

My own personal feelings are of gratitude for the "parents" devotion. I learnt how to mix with anyone, to count one's blessings, to feel some compassion for another's sorrows.

I learnt all the arts (or most) of cricket, football, hockey etc at that place and played them until quite late in life. Sport has been my most enjoyable leisure in life."

Peter Kemp, an only child, was born in 1925. His mother died within a few months and his father placed him in a convent home. After his father died, when Peter was six, an aunt took him into her home. The arrangement did not succeed and she handed him on to another family. In 1934, he went back to the aunt who then handed nine year old Peter to the Home in Woodford. In an interview, he recalled as follows.

"I remember being taken into the house where Mr White lived and had his office. He sent me for a medical to Dr Smith and when I returned I was kept in isolation for three weeks. Ma Hutchin took care of me. She was a fantastic person, a little lady, humpty back, very gentle, very firm, kind and fair. Ma looked after all your needs. When the older children had gone to Church on Sunday evenings, she got the younger ones in and read to us. You were closer to Ma at first. As you got older, you joined the family as it were and one of the workers, the sisters, would be in charge of you.

When I first went we used to sleep two in a bed.
So I would sleep with a bigger boy. As a little
boy I went to bed first and had to warm his side
and then move over when he came. I think
officials ruled it out of order so then we had to
have our own beds. We used to dry with the same
towel passed down. Then we all got our own
towel.

The workers were called sisters. There was a
sister Florrie, Eileen, Mary, Jean and Gladys.
They stayed for years and you got to know them.
They worked as a team under Ma. They all ate
together in Ma's dining room and then they served
us.

I knew I was an orphan and was different but I
never felt a stigma. Our hair was normal and we
were dressed in ordinary clothes so we didn't
stand out at school. We walked to the school
together but you walked with a friend and we were
all chatting so it wasn't too bad. Today if
children from a home walked together to school it
would be considered unusual. And the teachers
didn't treat us differently. I used to get jobs
like filling the ink-wells - which was a
privilege. The classes were much bigger and the
teaching more formal then.

On a typical day, the workers got you up at 7 a.m.
We washed and then sat down for breakfast in the
hall, boys on one side, girls the other. We used
to have four half slices of bread with margarine
or marmalade. Cocoa to drink. Then we went
upstairs for prayers for 20-30 minutes. Mr White
took this. He was quite a character. If anything
happened which he regarded as an answer to prayer
he kept us up to date. At Easter once we had so
many hot cross buns - somebody left about 4,000 -

we were having them in our soup. He told us stories about Easter and they changed with the season. Then he'd ask us to say a text, then one or two choruses or a hymn. Afterwards we went to school. We came home for lunch which could be stew, something with meat in it. The meals were adequate. Fridays we had fish. Once I was ill after herrings and the doctor decided I was allergic to fish so I had boiled eggs. You had to eat everything, even cabbage. But you could overcome that if you had Wellington boots you could slide it down in there. Afternoon, back to school. When we came home one of the good things was our play area outside the hall. We amused ourselves playing cricket or football or keeping white mice in little hutches. We collected stamps. All the boys played chess because Mr White used to play us. There was no homework in those days. We couldn't leave the grounds but that was fair enough - they were responsible for us."

Peter's description of life in the Home is confirmed by Herbert's son Victor. Born in 1920, Victor entered fully into the routine of the Home. He described a typical Saturday in the 1930s.

"Getting up time was a bit later on Saturdays but everyone still had a chore to do. Usually the girls inside, the boys outside. The girls did washing-up, sweeping, tidying the bedrooms. The boys would be in the old orchard with the piles of wood which dad got people to dump there. The boys chopped it and had to chop enough to last for a week. That's a lot of wood to heat water for washing clothes that went on from Monday to Saturday. The added incentive was that the team for the afternoon football or cricket match was chosen not from the best players but from those who put their shoulders into the work. In the afternoon, as well as the match, we would play other games. The girls liked rounders, hop-scotch, skipping. Some would go shopping for Ma.

In the evenings there would be more games, often organised. After the hall was opened, there was more inside activity like singing and P.E.. People came in to teach us and we put on shows which were superb and ended with the girls' lantern march. The boys were trained by a neighbour, Mr Wilson, and he would be immaculate, all in white. At one time a Christian boxer used to teach boxing but he always insisted it was for defence."

Judith Tell's background was very different from most of the other children. Born in 1924, her family had been relatively well-off. Her father even stood as a candidate for parliament at one general election. Unfortunately, his wholesale business failed and he went bankrupt in 1928 and Judith continues,

"He got a job in Kent when I was five. The following year he was out of work again. Mum tried to make do and we didn't realise that while she was giving us enough food she was not eating sufficient herself. I was asthmatic and caught the flu which I passed on to Mum. She seemed to recover. On the Monday evening she was in high spirits and danced around with us. In the early hours I woke to hear her gasping for breath. My older brother was told to get the doctor and he went on his bike. By the time he came it was too late - she was dead. It was so sudden.

We went back to London but my father could not cope with us. My older brother went to work in a green grocers and my other brother stayed with dad. He then took my sister, Vanessa, my youngest brother and me to grandmother's at Leytonstone. I was coughing blood and went to convalescence in Broadstairs. In the meantime, while my father was away on business and a week before Christmas, grandmother put the other two into the Home at Woodford. I came back and followed them in the July. I was seven.

The day I went it was pouring with rain. An aunt took me. I went up the steps and waited in the sitting room, Mr White came in and I felt afraid. But I was fortunate because my sister was there and she looked after me.

Ma Hutchin was lovely. She was a wonderful person, a wonderful Christian. Whenever I had asthma - and I had it badly - she would sleep there in the sick room with me and she would hold my hand and say, "Come on, fight it, fight it.", because I wanted to give in. She was a little hunch-backed lady yet she would go down in the middle of the night to get me a drink. She was fabulous. I don't know how we could have existed without Ma. I would like to have had her to myself. She made us all red coats with black facings. She made our dresses. I enjoyed it when I was ill because I got attention. She used to talk to me a lot. I would ask for a book when I was ill and she would bring it and I would read it within a day. I read the Bible through and through. Everyone who went there loved Ma.

Pa White was extremely strict but fair. He had a sense of humour. He was a man of great faith and a good speaker. He would take groups of older boys and girls to Tower Hill where he preached. He was a very good outdoor speaker. I particularly remember the Christmases. Mr White used to cut the turkey. We even had a wireless and heard the King's speech. Mr White was always at his best at Christmas."

COMPARISON WITH DR BARNARDO'S

The reflections of the former children give the flavour of what life was like in the Home in the inter-war years, but in order to evaluate the quality of care some comparison must be made with contemporary child care of that period. In the last chapter, the Home was considered in the light of the state's Poor Law. Here it will be considered with Dr. Barnardo's which was the foremost voluntary society looking after some 8,500 children. Interestingly, two of the largest Barnardo homes were close to the Woodford Home, one in Woodford itself and one in Barkingside.

Two former Barnardo children wrote well-known books about their experiences in these years. In *The Likes of Us,* G.V. Holmes describes movingly a happy childhood spent in a cottage in the Village Homes at Barkingside.[9] In *The King of the Barbareens,* Janet Hitchman details more varied events in and out of foster homes and institutions before moving to the same Village Homes.[10] These autobiographies, along with other histories of Barnardo's, provide yardsticks with which to compare the Children's Home and Mission.

Similarities. Both the Barnardo's Homes and the Home possessed devoted staff. The mothers, as they were called, in charge of the Barnardo cottages were mainly single women dedicated to the well-being of their children. To many it was less of a job and more of a vocation to which they felt called by God. G.V. Holmes thought the world of her Barnardo's mother and wrote,

> "I believe that, apart from a really natural home circle, complete in itself, "my world" provided the happiest and finest environment for the upbringing of homeless, neglected, or unwanted children... the great love which always surrounded us cannot really be expressed in words."[11]

She attributed this happiness to the love and care which flowed from the mother in charge of her. Janet Hitchman commented on the same mother,

"For a time she and I were at loggerheads and could only see each other's faults, but eventually respect and even a spark of love grew between us."[12]

At the Home, too, children had kindly relationships with dedicated women. Foremost was Ma Hutchin who knew every child. Her aunt, Fanny Hutchin, joined her at the age of 62 and stayed 19 years until her death in 1921. A few staff endured only a year or two but these years were marked by a stability amongst the sisters, as they were called. Amongst the devoted women were Lydia Lawrence, Edith Jones, Janet Jones, sister Minnie, sister Jessie and a Miss E. Allwright in the 1920s. Sister Maud Simmonds came in 1925 after training at Mount Hermon Missionary College and died, tragically young, after a throat operation in 1934. During the 1930s, the mainstays were Florrie Stockwell, Alice Coleman, Gladys Skiffins, Jean Morrow, Mary Runacres and the aforesaid Miss E.Allwright. They laboured long hours for about ten shillings a week. Like their counterparts at Barnardo's, they were motivated by something different from money.

With up to 80 children in the Home, the staff could not provide the close attention and contact of the parent of a small family. Thus Judith Tell sometimes longed to be cuddled or kissed by someone. It appears that the staff were careful not to develop favourites and not to build the very deep relationships which could not be sustained. Yet within this limited framework, the sisters strove to create an environment of fairness, affection and stability. Thus Harry Race recalled how he felt closest to sisters Jessie and Minnie while Judith Tell thought sister Jean was "marvellous".

In his history of child care in the first half of this

century, Nigel Middleton explains that in many institutions staff kept the children at a distance and, still influenced by the past, treated them "according to a formula that had been evolved for deterring the feckless and the work-shy."[13] Such a generalisation could not be applied to the staff at the Home or at Barnardo's. They both possessed dedicated female staff whose concern for their children was firm yet affectionate and combined with a commitment to stay with them.

Nigel Middleton also criticises many inter-war institutions for being "almost devoid of cultural amenities" so leading to "cultural and psychological deprivations."[14] Barnardo's and the Home were further similar in that both escape this criticism for their agencies provided adequate recreational activities. Certainly their inmates did not go to many concerts and plays but which working class children did? However, they did have access to a variety of leisure pursuits. At Barnardo's, encouragement was given to reading, stamp collecting and drawing and the girls could join the Brownies or Guides. At the Home in Woodford, football, cricket and netball was always available and, for a while, the children had access to a nearby private tennis court. For many of these years, helpers came in from outside to run clubs. Miss Fisher taught music which culminated in a public show. Miss Le Vierge and the appropriately named Miss Fitter took the girls for drill, a popular activity of the time, which again led to an annual display. The boys were taught by a Mr Sutton whose involvement must have extended beyond drill for he married one of the sisters. Day outings were a regular feature with Maldon, Clacton and Shoeburyness being popular venues. Later, the acquisition of Tiptree facilitated longer holidays.

But recreation was not all. In both Barnardo's and the Home the children were expected to contribute to the cleaning of the buildings. Taken in conjunction with the meals, it could be said that plain food and plentiful duties were characteristic of both regimes.

At Barnardo's, G.V. Holmes remembered, "Tea was plain, jam, sometimes dripping - water cress, sometimes cake."[15] Janet Hitchman adds that the porridge for breakfast was "a great mass (which) looked exactly like chicken food" and says that the meals were "awful" because they were cooked "by the house-girls as part of their training." She also explains that "Each of us, from eight years old upwards, had a household task to complete before breakfast. The baking tins had to be polished with emery paper and the floor underneath the bath hearth-stoned. The window-sills, doorsteps and surrounds of the drains were white-washed daily, whatever the weather."[16]

The recollections of former children at the Children's Home and Mission, as have been detailed earlier, also reveal the combination of household duties followed by plain but adequate diet. It should be interjected that these features were not unusual in residential establishments. Lucy Hayes, a prominent child care figure, ran a local authority home in the 1930s which became almost a model of what should be done. There the children rose at 7a.m. and completed certain domestic jobs.[17] The point being drawn out is that the standard of food at the Home and the practice of children participating in the upkeep of the buildings were in common with what went on in children's homes which had a high reputation.

Lastly, Barnardo's and the Home were similar in having strict regimes. On arrival, Janet Hitchman was warned that her mother "wallops with a hairbrush." The said mother ruled her cottage firmly. The children rose at 6.30 a.m., dressed in silence, and then undertook their tasks. Even outside the cottage, life was surrounded with rules with children being warned not to walk on the grass let alone wander outside the gates. As Janet remarked, "At Barnardo's, drawing breath was our only freedom and that had to be drawn silently."[18] Infringements of the rules were met by punishments. Yet slowly Janet perceived that a large institution could only function within a framework of rules and, as she did, so she developed a respect, even love, for the mother of her cottage.

At Woodford, too, the regime of the Home was strict with a timetabled day and rules which had to be observed. Ma Hutchin had a small cane which she hardly ever used. Peter Kemp recalled,

> "If you were naughty you had to stand outside Ma's room. Occasionally she or one of the workers might cane you on the hand. We accepted punishment provided it was fair."

Sometimes, too, Herbert would resort to the cane and Judith Tell recalls her brother receiving it after he ran away and herself being slapped by him.

Today corporal punishment is banned in all statutory and most voluntary children's homes. In regard to its use at Barnardo's and the Home, four points need to be made. First, at that time corporal punishment was the norm. Even in my school days in the 1940s, canning was common. Second, at Barnardo's and the Home the cane was not used excessively in the ways described by Middleton at some institutions.[19] Third, punishment was regarded as a means of instiling good habits deemed necessary to enable the children to cope in the outside world. Fourth, the punishments were within a context of care and affection.

Both Ma and Herbert maintained control more by the force of their personalities. Ma had a quiet dignity and "no nonsense approach." Herbert had a forceful, direct, manner. His method was to be very strict initially and then to relax as the children fitted in. Judith Tell was frightened when she first entered the Home and wanted to keep away from him. But she added that gradually she appreciated his kindness and humour. She recalled how Herbert once came across her reading the Bible and asked what part she liked. Judith told with some relish the incident where Job scraped his boils with a piece of pottery. Much amused, Herbert thereafter called her Job. Her sister, Vanessa, stated, "My first impression of Mr White was a frightening one. He got silence just by clearing his throat." Yet she added that she "soon got on with him very well after an initial conflict...Later he used to talk to me of his future plans and hopes for the Home." Vanessa particularly appreciated Herbert's concern for her health. He called her "a hot-house plant" and he sat with her and told her how brave she was during her treatment for rheumatic fever. She continued,

"Mr White and I respected each other. He asked me to, stay on as a worker and to come back. I said I would but the war came. He was a good man with a fierce expression but a twinkle in his eye."

Herbert's approach of initial strictness to persuade newcomers to adapt to the routine of the Home was similar to that at Barnardo's. It may well have caused some unhappiness to children in their early days. Yet whether for the up to 80 children at the Home or over 1000 at Barnardo's, rules and routines were necessary to keep the establishments running smoothly. It was as though the staff were saying, "Look, we're going to live together for a long time, let's get the rules understood right away and then we'll get on fine." As time went by, the staff relaxed, attitudes softened and respect and affection grew between them and the children.

Differences. Despite the similarities, a visit to Dr. Barnardo's and the Children's Home and Mission would have revealed striking differences. Most obvious was that of numerical size. G.V. Holmes joined 1,400 children and 300 staff living in 70 cottages at Barkingside. Such large numbers were not unique. Quarriers and Mullers had well over 1,000 children at their peaks. By contrast, the Home never went above 88 and, in these years, usually catered for 70-80.

Certainly, the Home received more applications than it could take and, for a while, serious consideration was given to expansion. In 1921, Herbert was offered an estate of nearly 11 acres complete with hospital, school and laundry and capable of coping with 300 children. Moreover, it was offered outright as freehold property whereas at the time the Home was in rented housing. A large institution might have put the Home on the national child care map and might have attracted many more donations. Yet, after prayer, the offer was declined. The reasons were never stated but they can be surmised as follows.

First, Herbert and his colleagues did not want the Home to be identified with a person as tended to happen with large and famous institutions. He was never critical of Barnardo's yet he would be uneasy with the way in which children were called a Barnardo's Boy or Barnardo's Girl. Within Woodford he discouraged any tendency to use the term White's Homes.

Second, they did not want fame and public recognition. The staff relied upon God not publicity for their resources.

Third, the smaller size of the Home was regarded as more appropriate to the creating of an atmosphere of home life. Today a home of 70 children would be considered very large. Not then. Herbert and his team thought it small enough to enable the children to develop relationships and for the staff to develop an atmosphere which was modelled on family life. The Rev. Louis Parkinson, the local Baptist minister who had a long association with Herbert, expressed this sentiment in 1930 when he was reported as stating,

> "...the one great feature that characterised the Home was that it gave the children of the Home a sense of security and love: whereas in some of those big public institutions that sense of security and love was missing. It meant that the Children's Home was a Home."

In the many letters received from former children, it is noticeable that nearly all referred not to White's Homes, not to the Children's Home and Mission but simply to "home".

Fourth, the smaller size made for closer ties with the local community. The enormous extent of the large institutions made them into worlds of their own. The Barnardo's Village Homes covered two square miles and, in addition to the rows of cottages, contained a receiving home, church, library, hospitals and laundry. Even the girl guides met inside the walls. At the Barnardo's Home in Woodford, the boys did eventually go to outside schools but the girls at Barkingside received all their education inside. Thus they had few contacts with life outside which, as Janet Hitchman made clear, was poor preparation for when they did have to leave.

The children in the Home by no means mixed freely with outsiders, probably did not have friendships with local children and certainly were not allowed to bring friends in. Thus there was a degree of isolation which will be discussed in a later chapter. But, at least, they lived in an ordinary street and opened the door to ordinary trades people. They went to local schools and often to local churches. The doctor, the optician, the dentist, the chiropodist were not specialists employed just within the institution but were professionals who also served the rest of the community. Neighbours were involved in running the music and drill clubs and the Sunday School when it started in the new hall. The children were sent by Ma to shop at the nearby grocers and post office. Outings were shared with children from other churches. The children from the Home were different, they knew it and the neighbourhood knew it. But they were also a part of the Woodford community. Herbert recognised the value of this link and realised it would be diminished by large numbers.

Another major difference was that the Home was mixed. The

two large and nearby complexes were divided according to sex. Indeed, siblings might be split so that brothers were in one institution and sisters in another. The girls in the Barkingside Village Home had female housemothers and female teachers. G.V. Holmes complained, "The gardeners and workmen...... represented practically the only male contacts."[20] The outcome, amusingly yet tragically recorded by Janet Hitchman, could be an ignorance about and difficulty in relating to men in later years.[21]

At least the Barnardo cottages had some babies and thus a wide age span. The Children's Home and Mission did not accept children until the age of about 7. The absence of babies, apart from those of the White family, must have militated against the intention to generate a family atmosphere. But the Home did contain both boys and girls, often including brothers and sisters. Further, there were some men around. True, the bulk of the day to day caring was in the hands of women but Herbert was seen daily, a former missionary, Mr Ellis was on the staff for a while, Ewart and Herbert White junior played an increasing part, and male instructors and Sunday School teachers came in from outside.

The mixture of boys and girls and the involvement of some men gave the children more opportunities to mix socially and emotionally with persons of the opposite sex. Victor White recalled,

> "The boys and girls got on well but rarely went out with each other. I remember Jim, an attractive lad, whenever someone asked him whether he went out with the girls he replied, 'No. They're my sisters'."

In the older age range, girls tended to outnumber boys. Both could leave school at fourteen years but the Home often retained the girls for a further two years in order to train them for service. The boys were more likely to go to work and live at no. 18 Crescent Road or be found digs.

However, the approach was flexible and no-one was pushed out just to fend for themselves. In some instances, children who were not coping outside were allowed to come back in for a while. To repeat, the Home could never replace the natural family unit but the mixture of the sexes, combined with the attitude that this was their home, did something to formulate a sense of family.

A difference not often appreciated is that the White family lived on the premises. Thomas Barnardo, Thomas Stephenson, Edward Rudolf and others were revered rightly as child care pioneers yet none of them actually shared in the daily life of the children. By the time G.V. Holmes and Janet Hitchman entered the Village Homes, the Governors were the Hon. Ann MacNaughton and Miss B. Picton-Turberill who were devoted leaders but ones rarely seen by the children.

By contrast, Herbert knew all the children in his care. He was often out preaching yet the children usually saw him at prayers in the morning and he liked to join in the games in the evening. In the summer he would place a penny on the centre one of three cricket stumps and then give it to children who could bowl him out. But it was not just Herbert. The whole family lived there -- Edith, of course, and the six children, Herbert junior, Olive, Ewart, Eunice, Victor and Edith junior.

The Whites dwelt in a separate house opposite the other houses in Crescent Road. Separate but small with only three bedrooms. The children mixed daily with the children of the Home and went to the same schools. As Olive White put it, "We never felt different. We played with the children and looked upon them as our brothers and sisters." Victor White recalled how the older boys protected him,

> "I can remember aged nine coming home from
> Churchfield School and a big lad, a bricky's son,
> pushed me and banged my head on the bridge.
> Leonard Want, one of the boys from the Home,
> challenged him, took off his glasses and jacket,

rolled up his sleeves and knocked him down. He
then took me by the hand and walked me home.
Later he taught me how to box."

Victor added that, sadly, Leonard contracted a bone-marrow
illness. The Home continued to care for him past school-
leaving age and sent him to convalescence in Margate but he
died aged 21. Victor was incorporated into the football
team and the friendships of the other children. So, in
contrast to the more famous child care figures, the Whites
were inside not outside the Home, were present not distant,
were daily participants rather than regular visitors. Far
from copying the established child care pattern, Herbert
White adopted some new approaches. He did so not because
they were new but because he saw them as suited to the needs
of the children.

One other difference should be recorded. The Children's
Home and Mission had no programme of fostering - or boarding
out, as it was often called - for its children. Today
fostering is a major means of providing care for children
separated from their own parents. Interestingly Judith Tell
and her husband became foster parents for a local authority
and, as a young child care officer in the early 1960s, I
used to visit their home. But prior to the second world war
fostering was not so well developed, although in Scotland a
high number of pauper children were fostered with crofting
families. Dr. Barnardo's along with other large voluntary
bodies was gradually expanding its use of foster homes
although the bulk of its care remained residential.

Why did Herbert White and his colleagues not promote
fostering at all? As they hardly ever refer to the topic,
save when finding digs for some older boys, it is hard to be
sure. However it is obvious that a system of fostering
would have required very different resources and skills than
those available to them. Further it is important to note
that fostering in the inter war years did not offer all the
advantages associated with it today. Nigel Middleton points

out its following defects:

> "the selection of foster parents left much to be
> desired with the result that unsuitable couples
> could lead to unhappy children and breakdowns of
> the placements:
> supervision of the foster homes was often
> inadequate:
> brothers and sisters were sometimes deliberately
> placed in different foster homes:
> some agencies had policies of removing the
> children from the foster homes at the ages of 12-
> 14 years and returning them to the residential
> establishments for training prior to employment:
> fostering was often regarded as a 'clean break'
> with little encouragement given to contact with
> natural parents."[22]

An example of unfortunate fosterings is found in Janet Hitchman's autobiography. She endured cruelties and rejections before settling in at the Village Home. This is not to deny that successful fosterings did occur but rather to show that they required careful selection of foster parents, appropriate matching of couples with child, and regular supervision. Whether Herbert and his staff acknowledged these factors and made a deliberate decision to concentrate on residential care is not known. It is certain that they opted for the security of long-term residential care which gave safety from ill-treatment, kept siblings together and allowed contact with natural parents where possible. This concentration made the Home different from other major child care societies which could offer more varied and diversified forms of looking after children. But, in the circumstances, it was a sensible course of action which made the best use of available resources and skills.

In order to put the Children's Home and Mission in its contemporary child care context, a comparison has been made with Dr. Barnardo's. Like Barnardo's, the Home possessed the advantages of devoted staff and varied recreational activities. As at Barnardo's, its children had to undertake household duties and endure plain food and a strict regime. Unlike Barnardo's, the Home did not possess the huge resources and facilities to offer multiple approaches, particularly fostering. None the less, its residential care had the advantages which spring from a smaller size, mixed composition and a leader who lived on the premises. Thus the Home emerges creditably even when considered beside the most famous child welfare agency of its day.

WHAT HAPPENED TO THE CHILDREN?

The experiences of some children within the Home, as told by themselves, and a comparison with children in another agency have now been recounted. But what happened to the children after they left the Home? Of course, some children stayed just short periods before returning to parents or other relatives who had recovered from illness, found employment or re-married. Many, however, stayed at the Home until they left school. Unless they too could go to relatives, they faced a future without any obvious place to live. What then?

The majority of girls went into service, that is they became maids. Domestic service was the most widespread occupation amongst unmarried working class women in Britain in the first part of this century. My grandmother was a maid whose duties included ironing out any creases in the morning newspapers. The post was poorly paid, entailed long hours and few holidays. Why did she do it? Because, coming from a large family, she needed a job which supplied accommodation. The major advantage of service was its residential component. Consequently, girls not just from the Home but from Barnardo's, National Children's Home, Quarriers etc. commonly became maids and remained so until they married.

Herbert and Ma were aware of the dangers of service.

Unsuitable girls were soon sacked. Unscrupulous employers could exploit maids both financially and sexually. Living-in jobs tended to make the girls isolated and, if they did not get on with those around them, unhappy. To try to counter these dangers, the staff at the Home adopted two practices. One was that the girls were not sent straight into service at the age of 14. Instead they were kept on at the Home for two years training. Of course, this training also provided a source of unpaid labour for the Home. Unpaid that is until representations from Judith Tell led to the introduction of a small wage. But, at least, the two years spent in training also enabled the girls to grow in maturity. The other practice was that Herbert personally sought out and vetted posts for them. Here his many contacts with church people, particularly vicars in large houses, provided a useful source of employment.

Martha Surrey entered service soon after the first world war. She went as a parlour maid to a family at Buckhurst Hill with a wage of £12 a year. She remembers with humour how she waited at table one day,

> "They had an important gentleman to dine. Their
> bulldog got in the room and I started calling the
> dog by name, 'Consul, get out, Consul, get out'.
> The funny thing was that the man was a consul, and
> thought I was calling him."

Martha never really liked service but stuck it for some years. Fortunately, Buckhurst Hill is near Woodford so she was able to maintain frequent contact with the staff and other friends at the Home.

Some years later, Vanessa Tell went into service in Putney. Her sister, Judith, says she was "hopeless" and made mistakes like standing a hot iron on the wooden window sill. Yet Vanessa possessed a charm and cheerfulness which preserved her when others would have received the boot. Judith explained,

> "She had a bell over her bed and was supposed to

make tea for the family when it rang. She just turned it off and, in the end, the lady of the house came up and brought her a cup of tea. My sister got away with anything."

This family owned the Sunlight Laundry in Brixton and Vanessa persuaded them to give her a job there. They agreed so Vanessa was able to leave service and rent herself some rooms where later she was joined by Judith. Judith's asthma had - to her delight - curtailed her domestic training. She went to classes in shorthand and typing and obtained a post with the General Accident Insurance Company.

Unlike Judith and Vanessa, most girls did not move out of service so easily. Some enjoyed the work and were treated so kindly by the families that long-standing bonds of loyalty and affection were formed. Others could not wait for the day, and it took a long time, when they had saved enough to rent lodgings and seek alternative employment. But, at least, the girls were assured of the continued interest of Herbert, Edith and Ma. Letters were exchanged. The girls could spend their days off and their holidays at the Home. And if they lost one job then Herbert was prepared to help them find another. In contrast to the Poor Law, which wanted to save money by accepting no responsibility for youngsters once they left the doors, the Home maintained close ties with the young people whom they still regarded as a part of the family.

Herbert was keen to find a trade for boy leavers. These were difficult economic years and jobs were hard to come by. As early as 1904, Herbert attempted to establish a tea and coffee business as a source of employment. Nothing more was heard of it so presumably it did not survive. Some leavers did obtain apprenticeships as carpenters, joiners, watchmakers and so on. The drawback was that the wages of apprentices were so low that it was difficult for them to survive financially without the support of parents. Consequently, a number of leavers sought careers in the armed forces as boy entrants. The positive aspect was that the army or navy ensured somewhere to live, some security of income and often a training in a trade. The negative side was that the boys were again entering institutional life and so gaining no experience of life within a small family.

There was one other outlet - emigration. Both the Poor Law and the major child care societies organised an exodus of children to Canada, Australia, New Zealand and South Africa. Between 1869 - 1919, over 73,000 children went to Canada unaccompanied by parents. The flow was not in the same numbers between the wars but still many children went.

Undoubtedly some children made successful careers and created happy homes abroad and a few made a fortune. Generally, however, the emigration schemes have come under heavy criticism. Once in out-lying farms, children were often exploited as cheap labour. Visits from supervisors were rare. The young people, as they became, were often paid poor wages and provided with no marketable skills. Some were desperately lonely and unhappy.

The numbers of children who emigrated from the Home were very few. Certainly there was no policy, no organised scheme for sending them abroad. Harry Race said that, when he developed an interest, he went to Herbert for his advice. Herbert discussed it with him but left the decision with Harry. Herbert then told him how he should apply to Canada House. Emigration was a fact of life in this era and certainly some children from the Home did go abroad. Of these it is impossible to say how they all fared. However, sometimes letters appeared in *Links*. Two were published in 1929. One writer said,

"I am getting on fine and am contented with my place - I have learnt a lot since I have been here and feel as though I could manage a farm myself."

The other wrote,

"I would like you to tell the boys and girls that

they had better hurry up and come to Canada to earn their living. I go to Church on an Indian horse. There is plenty of work and I am glad of it."

The 1930 issue contained letters from a couple, both of whom had been in the Home, in Australia and more from Canada. One penned,

"I am getting along fine. Am working on a hundred acre farm. I attend Sunday School regularly and attend church every two weeks... All of us boys owe our chance of success in this country to the care you gave us. Scarcely a day passes but what we are reminded in some way of the patient and painstaking training you gave us in the old land."

These letters, and others like them, may not be truly representative of the experiences of all those who emigrated from the Home. Clearly, some youngsters stayed just for a short period before returning. One such was Harry Race who at the age of 16 found himself working on a farm in Quebec for a few dollars a month plus board. After two and a half years, he took the train to Montreal and sought out a hostel. To his amazement the door was opened by a boy he had known in the Home. Harry subsequently laboured on another farm before working his passage back to Britain. After months of unemployment, he worked in the car industry and then as a waiter before joining the air force in which he served as aircrew during the second world war. After the war, he built upon his experience to become a licensed air engineer and took posts in Canada and Australia before returning to Britain. Harry did eventually settle in Britain. Others stayed abroad. Interestingly, years later in the 1980's Victor and Margaret White made a world tour visiting many former residents of the Home.

Harry Race must have been a resourceful person. Whatever the boys did on leaving the Home they tended to have two pluses. One was that they had been taught to put their hands to a variety of tasks. As Herbert wrote in 1919, "Quite a feature of the work is that our children are taught to be useful in sewing, cleaning, shopping, boot repairing etc which will greatly assist them in days to come." The other was that they acquired habits which would go down well with prospective employers, habits like tidiness, punctuality and politeness. For instance, Herbert always advised against smoking. In 1927, a boy wrote from Canada saying that a farmer came to the hostel looking for a farm hand. He chose the one who had no nicotine stains on his hands. The boy stated to Herbert, "I have got my first job in Canada by taking your advice."

It was mentioned that contact was maintained with girls who went into service. But it was not just with them. The files were full of correspondence with leavers of all kinds. Periodic re-unions were organized with, for instance, 50 former children coming together in March, 1921. To cite too many letters from leavers would be repetitive but here are four examples from 1937. One from a boy who left the Home in 1928, went to Canada and then came back to live in Potters Bar. He wrote,

"I shall always call it my Home where ever I be. Please give my kind wishes and an orphan's love to Miss Hutchin (she was a true Mother to me) and to the sisters."

The second from an old girl reported that,

"I am getting on nicely and have had a 2s rise. Can you arrange for me to be baptised as soon as possible for I want people to know that I am out and out for Christ."

The third was from a boy, who left over 20 years before, thanking the Home for allowing him to return for the previous Christmas. He wrote,

"It was a wonderful experience and one I shall not soon forget. It brought memories crowding back again."

The fourth from an old boy looking forward to the next Christmas. He asked,

> "May I come down and spend Christmas with you. I have so enjoyed the past days and pray that God will continue to supply your needs. Thank you for all your kindness."

As early as 1919, Herbert said. "One of our greatest joys is that when our children leave us for work and service, we do not lose sight of them. They constantly 'Come Home' showing how much they appreciate what has been done." Whatever happened to the children in their later jobs and home lives, there is no doubt that the staff of the Home continued to offer interest, advice and concern.

HERBERT UNDER PRESSURE

These inter-war years saw the Home grow in terms of numbers of children, staff and buildings. The wider family expanded as leavers continued their relationships with what they regarded as their home. The impression might be given that Herbert just sailed through all this. The onlookers at the annual meetings might have thought that this jolly, smiling man had divine protection from the stresses, temptations and worries that beset ordinary mortals.

Far from it. For a start, Herbert had his detractors, those who considered him a crank or who resented his forceful leadership. His grandson, Keith, explains that the moves to have Herbert conscripted during the war were inspired by local men who disliked him.[23] Then there was the sheer enormity of the task. As the director of the Home, he felt for each child. The health of the children was usually good: even so the occasional death, for instance that of 10 year old Jean Moore in 1920 following appendicitis, affected him deeply. As director, his was the final responsibility for the education, feeding, safety and behaviour of up to 80 children. The reality of the load is underlined if it is pointed out that in some institutions children were poorly educated, underfed and physically abused. Official inspections of voluntary homes were erratic partly because the duty was fragmented between several statutory departments. None the less, they did occur and children's homes could be publicly criticised and even closed down. In the case of the Home, official visits had led to reductions in the numbers of children taken and changes in the sleeping arrangements. Communications with officials were a source of strain to Herbert to the extent that the arrival of an envelope from the Home Office or like body caused him to depart from his usual custom of opening all the post himself. He would hand the letter to Edith who would then summarise the contents to him as positively as possible.

In addition to the heavy responsibility for the Home, Herbert also carried a weighty physical load. He rose early, spent some time with his own family, usually led morning prayers with the Home's children, dealt with the over-sight and administration and, in the evening, tried to participate in activities with the children. Further, he was constantly preaching. As will be demonstrated in the next chapter, he was much in demand as an evangelist. As early as 1919, he spoke at 29 different places in 12 months at a time when he was still working in the munitions factory. It was not as though he took regular holidays. In 1920, Ma Hutchin and Olive White had a break at Folkestone, Edith and one daughter went to Westcliff, two of the White boys holidayed at Brighton and some of the sisters to other places. But not Herbert.

The White family was a source of joy to Herbert and Edith with Victor in 1920 and Edith junior (known as Bunty) in 1924 being added to them in these years. Yet Herbert junior and Eunice suffered constant ill-health. Following an accident with a horse, Herbert junior was in a coma for 10 months and never fully recovered. Eunice was someone special, blessed with a sweet disposition and a deep spirituality. At the age of 10, she was diagnosed as having a valvular disease of the heart and a perforated ear-drum. The following 12 years saw her in frequent pain which she bore patiently until her death on September 7th, 1936. For Herbert and Edith, having done so much for other children, the loss of their own girl must have been a shattering blow. Edith appeared to cope the better. She grieved profoundly yet calmly accepted that all was in God's hands. Herbert reeled from the shock. Olive heard her agitated father pacing up and down in his office repeatedly muttering "The work must go on."

These pressures took their toll and Herbert experienced bouts of illness. Interestingly, in his autobiography, George Muller - whose principles and practices were followed by Herbert - revealed that he went through periods of serious illness, particularly following the death of his son.[24] In Herbert's case, it seems he suffered from nervous exhaustion. At the annual gathering of 1924, Dr Flegg issued him a mild rebuke for not taking more rest. Herbert did not heed the advice and thus, at times, paid the price when exhaustion forced him to rest. The remarkable factor is that he would recover and then continue and expand his activities. The question arises, how did Herbert survive in these busy inter-war years?

Already it will be evident that Herbert's personal qualities were exceptional. He might be knocked down but he got up when other people would have stayed down. More of his qualities at a later stage. But he could not have coped alone and, as indicated in the previous chapter, he was blessed in the contributions made by others. Ma Hutchin continued as the everyday, dependable rock and also marshalled the helpers - the sisters - into a loyal team. The sisters worked long hours. Martha Surrey, who returned to work in the Home, commented, "It was hard work. I did much of the cooking on a big oven with two iron doors. If we wanted time off we had to ask permission. But we all got on well together. It was a happy time." Ma and the sisters were ever present and without that service the care of the children would have been impossible.

In addition, the safety, well-being and health of the children continued to attract the support of local professional people. During these years a dentist gave his services and Herbert, probably tongue in cheek, publicly thanked him for "taking great pains to keep the mouths of our children in good order." Then an optician and a chiropodist added their expertise. Dr Martin Flegg officially retired in 1930 and was presented with a clock. In response the good doctor said his reward had been the "wonderful improvement" in the children's health. Then, as usual, he diverted attention from himself by wishing "that Mr White would write a book on the way in which God answered prayer."

In fact, God immediately supplied a medical replacement. Another local general practitioner, Dr David Smith offered his services backed up, from 1934, by his assistant Dr Eric Mathie. They soon showed themselves as capable doctors although, if in doubt, they could still turn to Dr Flegg for consultation. In fact, 1933-34 proved a difficult year with 10 cases of diptheria and one of scarlet fever. Otherwise the health record was amazingly clean even when mumps, measles and whooping cough were sweeping the district. In 1937, Dr Mathie reported that "the health of the children had been remarkably good while the health of the people of Woodford had been conspicuously bad." He attributed this outcome partly to the children's diet, partly to the high standards of care from the staff.

Unsung but just as important to the well-being of the Home were the practical contributions of friends. In 1930, Ma thanked one sewing party which had made 1476 garments since 1915. By 1934, there were eight such sewing groups, two Boot Clubs which saved money for footwear, and a friend who came in regularly to mend the boots and shoes. Others decorated rooms or painted outside - all free of charge. In his low days, Herbert must have been encouraged to look up and see a supporter painting a window sill or a man mending another hole in a boot.

It was not just friends. At times, Herbert may have worried about his family members but overall they upheld him. The warm and happy relationship with his wife and children must have been a fount of emotional strength. Further, they nearly all played practical roles in the running of the Home. In this respect, the part of Herbert's wife, Edith, deserves special attention. It can best be done in the words of two of her children. Olive recalled,

> "Mum was very quiet and strong. A remarkable woman. Yes meant yes, no meant no. She never complained about dad going off for three weeks in the caravan preaching. She held the fort. There was a real closeness. She backed dad completely. You never heard mum and dad complain about lack of money."

The presence in the Home of Ma Hutchin, one of the founders, and Edith, who arrived later as Herbert's wife, might have resulted in rivalry and conflict. Yet Victor White explained that they worked out a good relationship based on an acceptance of each other's roles. Ma had the charge of the day to day care of the children. Edith, a trained typist, ran the office as well as looking after her family. It worked well.

As a young child, Victor White enjoyed the warmth of his mother's love and nearness. He even appreciated being ill when she lit a fire in the bedroom and made a lot of fuss of him. He stated,

> "She was the main strength of it all. She was the one who took us for prayers when we went to bed - father was out so much - she ran the home. She was physically frail. Never swam in her life and took heart tablets. She was very regal, quiet,

never raised her voice. Totally reliable and always even in her judgement. The opposite to father who was impulsive, dynamic, he went up and down, roaring laughter or tears.

She never showed any resentment. Father was always bringing people in for supper. One evening he brought in four. Olive bristled and said, 'The only food is for tomorrow's dinner'. Mum replied, 'You have a lot to learn, my love.' We had dinner and the next evening mum said to Olive, 'Did we have dinner? Yes.'"

Herbert and Edith possessed very different personalities and abilities. Yet the differences bound them together rather than dis-uniting them. These varied features also benefited their children as can be illustrated by the way they dealt with two crises in Victor's life. As a teenager, Victor fell for a beautiful girl, Margaret, at George Lane Baptist Church. After a while, Margaret told him they were not suited. Victor was devastated and poured out his feelings to his mum. Victor recalls that after listening she said,
    "Now Victor, you have trusted your life to Jesus? 'Yes'. Then trust Him for friendships. If you keep close to Him, He'll work it out."
Victor was impressed by his mother's calm concern and took her advice. For some months they hardly spoke to each other but, when they did, it was with a view to a serious relationship and they later married.

Not so long afterwards, Victor was employed at an import and export firm in a minor clerical position. The second world war came and many staff members were conscripted. The boss told Victor he would have to be in charge of exports. Feeling unable to cope, he decided to leave and went and told dad. Herbert promptly reared up and retorted,
    "You're not. You're a coward. You go back. You can never tell until you've tried."
Victor went back, took on the new responsibilities and made

a success of them.

Edith listened and then gave measured and thoughtful advice. Herbert roared and refused to listen to excuses. Both were effective in different situations and both responses revealed the parents' different characters. It is easy to see the charismatic Herbert as the stronger character. Certainly, he was the man of vision, faith and daring. Yet from the mountain tops he could descend into the valleys. Edith too had steel in her make-up. She never gave up, never for a moment tried to persuade Herbert to do something easier. And when Herbert was ill, particularly in 1923, it was Edith who nursed him and took over some of his duties. If she had steel, she also had softness. She was always there for her children who all loved and admired her. And not just her own. Edith knew the children of the Home and, when they left, she was the one who maintained communication through hundreds of letters. The story of the Home is not just that of Herbert White - it is also that of Edith White. As Olive put it, "Dad could not have done it without her."

Herbert was often away from his family. There are signs that his children sometimes resented that their dad had less time for them because he was so devoted to other people's children. Yet the love of Herbert and Edith appeared to overcome any resentment so that it changed into understanding and then into shared involvement. Another reason why Herbert was able to endure, was that he had the support of his children. Both Herbert junior and Ewart are listed as helpers in the 1930s although the former never enjoyed abundant health. Victor was eventually to take over from his father as leader. In addition, all through these years Olive was playing her part. On leaving school in the early 1920s, she worked outside in an office for a few months then, with Herbert junior and Eunice occupying much of Edith's time, she took over much of the care of the family. And in the 1920s, with few mechanical cleaning appliances, that was hard work. Mondays was wash day and Olive got up very early to light the boiler. At 7.30 she took a cup of tea to mum. On top of this, she gave some of her time to nursing babies Victor and Bunty. Olive married in 1948 and eventually took over much of the work in Abridge which will be explained in the next chapter. After her husband's death in 1955 she returned to work full-time in the Home. In the 1990s, she still lives there and remains as bright and committed as ever. To her and the other White children, the giving of time to the Home was not an irksome chore but eventually became a joyous duty. The willingness of both Edith and the children to support the cause must have been a major reason why Herbert was able to continue even when under pressure.

"HITHERTO HATH THE LORD HELPED US"

The inter-war years witnessed many changes at the Home. The premises expanded. The number of children multiplied. The White family grew up. Staff members changed. Two factors did not change - the participants' faith in God and God's provision.

In 1919, the Home started the year with a mere £2-17s-0¼d Yet the forthcoming twelve months saw all needs met. In the year, 1920-21, income was £1359-8s-9½d while expenditure was £1340-10s-0d. For 1925-26, income was £1644-15s-2¾d while expenditure was £1599-6s-1½d. The story remained the same. The amounts received always just covered the amounts required. Further, the contributions, all unsought, continued to come in small gifts. Thus in 1928-29, the receipt of £1887-7-0d came from 874 sources, an average of just over £2 per person. Even in 1933-34, a difficult economic year for Britain when other charities were recording a drop in giving, the Home experienced its highest ever income of £2114.

The financial figures do not reveal the full extent of giving to the Home for so many gifts came in kind. In 1920, Herbert stated that ever since 1916 56lb of fresh fish had arrived twice a week from Billingsgate fish market. Never one to waste material, he added that the boxes made excellent firewood. At Easter time, hot cross buns usually arrived. On one Good Friday breakfast there were still no buns. Still, Herbert said grace and gave thanks for them. Just as they were finishing the meal, a van drew up and delivered 4000 buns. At Christmas time, turkeys were required. In 1929, Herbert asked God for three turkeys. By Christmas Eve, only one had been given. The same evening, as late as 9.30 p.m., a friend called into a shop in Ilford to buy some cakes for the Home. The managing director of the shop happened to hear him talking about the children and promptly gave him two turkeys as well. The following year, the growing numbers fed well on five turkeys and two geese although, again, they did not appear until the day before Christmas. Fish, meat, vegetables, cocoa and so on - it all came.

It was not just food. In 1918-19, soap and envelopes were in very short supply following the war. Four cwts of soap followed by 4000 envelopes were delivered. The staff could only marvel and thank God. In 1924, the harmonium broke down beyond repair after years of constant use as children sung hymns and choruses. Very shortly after a phone message was communicated, "There's a piano being left with you tomorrow. Don't send it away." It came.

There is no doubt that Herbert wanted a car. It was not that he was interested in mechanical things rather that motorised wheels would facilitate the Lord's work. During these years, car ownership was not widely spread but in 1927 a friend donated money to purchase a second hand car. Herbert's choice of an Oakland model did not appear wise for it soon succumbed to the frost and he could only get 30 shillings for it as old iron. An old Wolseley had a similar brief existence before another friend from St Albans donated a second hand Austin. For some years, the Austin covered thousands of miles as it conveyed children, goods and Herbert himself.

Herbert's love-hate relationship with the Austin laid the grounds of his lasting and laughing reputation which became almost mythical in the eyes of Woodford residents. Former children delight to tell of the spluttering noises - both from the car and Herbert - as he strove to get the vehicle started. Then they were summoned out to push it down Crescent Road before he disappeared in a cloud of smoke and dust. He was, Harry Race chuckled, "the world's worst driver" who drove as though the road belonged to him. The children loved to go with him but needed nerves of iron as Herbert swerved, braked and kangarooed along. Further, he neglected car maintenance, oil, water and even petrol. He just expected cars to go. Somehow he did usually reach his destination.

Eventually even the Austin sank under the triple burden of heavy loads, high mileage and Herbert's driving. He wrote in January 1939,

"We have been praying for the Lord to touch someone to send another. Last Saturday, I had a phone call from the same friend saying, 'Keep in on Monday morning as the Lord has led me to give you a 1939 Hillman Minx.' This arrived at 11 a.m. and was left in exchange for the Austin together with the money to pay licence and insurance - Hallelujah!"

These incidents are perhaps the more dramatic and even amusing examples of God's provisions. But they were not isolated cases for all through these years the *Links* magazine continued to publish a diary showing what came in on a daily basis. The diaries fill pages, so here it must suffice to instance just two days in January, 1932.

"Jan 4. Waltham Cross, a load of wood. Seven Kings, 60 tins fruit, salmon, soup, coffee, cocoa, 20 jellies, 2 jars jam, 1 jar pickles, 14 pkts oats, pkt muffets, 3 pkts peas, 7 jars honey, 5 pkts wheat flakes, 2 bottles sweets, 3 pkts cornflour, 25 pkts soup, 19 pkts bisto, 3 pkts Bird's custard, 3 tins fruit salad and 6 tins spice.

Jan 5. Leyton 3s, M.P. 2s-6d. Beckenham £1. Spruce Hill Baptist C.E., 'I have much pleasure in sending 32s which is the proceeds of singing carols on Christmas Eve and the offerings at the service the following day.' Walthamstow £1. London, 56 lbs fish."

Goods did not arrive every single day, but most days saw the post or personal callers leaving postal orders, clothes and food. God's way of giving, as in the pre-1919 years, was through the continual donations of ordinary people and small churches. And their giving always rose in proportion to the need. At the head of one of the 1930 issues of *Links*, Herbert put, "Hitherto hath the Lord helped us." The Lord who helped them look after one child was still providing enough for over 80.

Not only was the Lord providing, He was going before them. In the autumn of 1939, war was declared between Britain and Germany. The threat was of large scale bombing of urban areas. The Home would have had to be evacuated. Tiptree was now ready. Herbert could only marvel and cite from God's Word,

"Before you call I will answer, and while you are yet speaking I will hear."

References

1. G. Lansbury, *My England,* Selwyn and Blount, 1934, p. 99
2. W. Beveridge, *Full Employment in a Free Society,* Allen & Unwin, 1944
3. N. Middleton, *When Family Failed,* Gollancz, 1971, p. 147
4. B. Holman, *Good Old George: The Life of George Lansbury,* Lion, 1990, p. 47
5. N. Middleton, *op.cit.,* p. 182
6. J. Stroud, *13 Penny Stamps,* Hodder and Stoughton, 1971, p. 174
7. D. Haynes, *Haste Ye Back,* Jarrolds, 1973
8. T. Fergusson, *Children in Care - and After,* Oxford University Press, 1966, chapter 1
9. G.V. Holmes, *The Likes of Us,* Frederick Muller Ltd, 1948
10. J. Hitchman, *The King of the Barbareens,* Penguin, 1960
11. G.V. Holmes, *op.cit.,* pp. 5-6
12 J. Hitchman, *op.cit.,* p. 150
13. N. Middleton, *op.cit.,* p. 267
14. N. Middleton, *op.cit.,* p. 265
15. G.V. Holmes, *op.cit.,* p. 12
16. J. Hitchman, *op.cit.,* pp. 150-51
17. L. Hayes, *Childrens Homes and the Deprived Child,* pamphlet, Hillcroft College, 1944
18. J. Hitchman, *op.cit.,* p. 149
19. N. Middleton, *op.cit.,* pp. 175-76
20. G.V. Holmes, *op.cit.,* p. 35
21. J. Hitchman, *op.cit.,* chapter 9
22. N. Middleton, *op.cit.,* chapter 10
23. K. White, *A Place for Us,* Mill Grove, 1976, p. 48
24. D. Matisko (ed.), *The Autobiography of George Muller,* Whitaker House, 1984, pp. 66-68

Mrs Florence Barclay

Opening of the Florence Barclay Memorial Hall, 1928

ALEC ELDRIDGE

BEN CLARKE

HENRY RANSOME

WALTER COE

Four boys who left for Canada in 1928

Girls Drill Squad, 1937

Boys Football Team, 1937

IV. The Evangelist

When the title, The Home for Destitute and Motherless Children, was dropped, it was replaced, not by The Children's Home, but by The Children's Home and Mission. The word Mission reveals that Herbert and his colleagues saw their work as having a double-fold purpose - the care of children *and* the spread of the Gospel.

This double-fold task was seen even more clearly in the work of George Muller, whose example was an inspiration to Herbert. In his diary of November 5th, 1835 - while he was still contemplating his life's work - Muller wrote,

"I certainly desire to be used by God to help the poor children...But the primary objective of the work is that God would be magnified because the orphans under my care will be provided with all they need through prayer and faith. Everyone will see that God is faithful and hears prayer." [1]

Herbert White's desire to open a Home was probably stimulated initially by the plight of the children he saw. But his decision was closely linked with his belief that, as he was obeying God, the resources would be provided by Him. In turn, this divine provision was proof of God's existence and activity which could be proclaimed to convince unbelievers. Dr Martyn Lloyd-Jones later explained,

"God's honouring of his faith in the matter of the Home was just a marvellous argument for the Evangelist to use because the world is in a state of unbelief." [2]

Herbert felt a burden to preach Jesus Christ, that is, to be an evangelist. He was convinced that people's eternity depended upon them accepting Jesus Christ as their Saviour. Therefore he took every opportunity to tell them. As a young man at the bank, he made no secret of his Christianity. Later, his son Victor recalled "being challenged at prayer-time as to whether any of us had spoken to the postman or milkman." As Victor put it, "He had a passion for souls." At a football match (father and son sometimes went to watch Tottenham Hotspur) Victor observed Herbert looking around and muttering as to how many of the fans were Christians. He half expected his dad to jump on the pitch and preach to the crowd.

THE PREACHER

And Herbert did preach to the crowds. He was not concerned to mount the pulpit in cathedrals. He wanted to reach those who were outside the Gospel. In the early years of the Home, he spent his holidays on Gospel tours. One, probably in 1909, was with his friend Fred Sackett. Starting in Ramsgate, they went to Margate, Broadstairs, Birchington, Southwood and Canterbury. They would pitch a tent and preach in the open air. On Margate sands it commenced to rain. As people drifted away, the young evangelist told them to stay and said he would ask the Lord to stop the rain. Herbert recorded, "This remark caused the crowd to laugh, but having prayed loudly to this effect, the rain instantly stopped until the close of our meeting. Thus our gracious Lord answered our prayer much to the amazement of the people." At Canterbury, conversions were made and help given to those with problems in their Christian lives. Herbert amusingly noted that he counselled a maid whose sin was that she swore at the cat which broke a dish in her pantry.

The two friends then adjourned to the Kentish hop fields where thousands of Londoners were picking the hops. They worked alongside the pickers in the day-time and then invited them to the evening meetings. On the last night, Fred appealed for decisions and Herbert rejoiced that 20 adults "came out on the Lord's side."

Fred Sackett went on to work for the Open Air Mission. Probably through this contact, Herbert became an honorary evangelist with them. As Victor White stated, "His special gift was open air work." His enthusiasm, loud, clear voice, earthy illustrations, and courage, made him ideal for this medium. He preached at race courses, outside railway stations, in the streets, indeed anywhere where crowds gathered. Once he was in Portsmouth when workers streamed out of the docks. Seeing a fruit seller, Herbert promptly bought his stock and hired the barrow. Jumping onto it, he then proclaimed the Gospel. His regular beats were at Tower Hill and Hyde Park where, in competition with other speakers and hecklers, he regularly preached to those who worked in the City.

It was not just in the open air. Herbert would go anywhere. The first World War opened up opportunities to visit army camps and address men in the barracks - if they would listen. On one occasion, he preached inside a barrack room until some soldiers grabbed him and threw him out of the window. Although bruised and somewhat fearful, Herbert dusted himself down and went back in. The same soldiers made for him again, but a sergeant intervened. He reasoned that if Herbert had the guts to return, then he had something important to say.

As his speaking reputation grew, so did invitations to speak in churches. In 1929-30, he was at 39 different churches (sometimes more than once) as well as at 12 different open air sites. The following year, he took services at 83 churches. Even in 1947-48, at the age of 69, he spoke at 35 churches. Noticeably, Herbert White's ministry was not usually at popular churches in prosperous middle-class areas. His diary was full of engagements at places like Dagenham Baptist Church, Kentish Town Mission, Marsh Street Mission, Grange Road Hall in Ilford, the Welcome Mission in Leytonstone, East Ham Mission, the Lighthouse Mission in Canning Town, and so on.

Herbert would not have been at ease in intellectual places of worship. He had not studied theology, and could not read

Hebrew or Greek. So what was it that made him such a sought-after speaker? First, he knew the Bible, its stories, miracles, parables, themes and doctrines. His talks were centred on the Biblical message and hence had a focus and consistency. Second, he had what can only be called style. Victor White recalled,

"He used to have missions - he'd take on a cinema and be billed as 'the man who has answers to prayer'. He'd launch into a racy story and then, bang, the cross. He was not a theologian, not a Spurgeon or a Lloyd-Jones, but he knew the word."

One of Herbert's favourite means of drawing a crowd was to place his hat on the ground and tell passers-by that it contained something alive. When some gathered around, he would lift the hat to reveal a Bible, the living word of God. Then he would preach.

Third, Herbert possessed a gift - priceless in the open air - of repartee. Once he told a crowd that God had answered his prayers by giving him a watch. When hecklers shouted to him to prove it, he promptly got out his watch. Another time, someone yelled out that he was cracked. He replied immediately, "That's right. That's how the light got in. I only hope that the light will get into your life too."

How effective was Herbert's preaching? Certainly he attracted crowds both indoors and out. Certainly he made a powerful impression. One resident of Tiptree wrote, "I can remember listening enthralled when he spoke at our church about the way God answered prayer and rewarded the faith of staff and children by providing for their needs. I decided that a God like that must be worth serving." Herbert's son, Victor, and grandson, Keith, still meet people who tell that they not only heard him preach, but can recall what he said. But for Herbert the test would be whether his preaching was used as a medium through which God changed lives. The evidence is strong that it did. In 1939, James Stokes was a young office worker, devastated by the recent death of his father. Wandering around Tower Hill, he stopped at the banner of the Open Air Mission. He heard Herbert declare, "I believe there is someone in the crowd who knows something about what I have been saying. If that is so, why don't you come up here and make your testimony?" To James' consternation, Herbert White suddenly looked straight at him and said, "I think that young chap down there knows something, don't you? Well, come up here and tell us about it." James went up and it was the start of a life-long friendship in which James became a supporter and trustee of the Home. By persuading James to witness, Herbert strengthened him and gave him the courage and desire to serve God more actively. Others were to follow in James' footsteps. Even more important to Herbert were those who responded for the first time to God's call. Once Herbert was speaking outside a pub in Bedford when a drunken man grabbed him by the coat and shouted, "If you won't stop, will you dance?" Herbert agreed, and as they danced, continued to give out tracts. At least the incident attracted a larger crowd including a young soldier, Keith Mitchell, who intervened to free Herbert. Afterwards, he went up to thank Keith. The conversation deepened and lengthened and concluded when the soldier there and then became a Christian. Soon after, he was killed in active service. Again, at one of the Tower Hill meetings stood a man who had just walked out on his wife. Their children had died in an epidemic and subsequently their marriage had deteriorated. That day he put the assurance policies where his wife would find them and left, determined to throw himself in the Thames. He paused at Tower Hill where Herbert's message of a God who could forgive and reconcile seemed just for him. Silently, he asked this God to take over his life and his problems. Returning home, he told his wife what had happened. She scoffed and retorted, "We'll wait and see." The husband asked her to look under a cushion where she found the assurance policies. They did wait and see and, in time, were reconciled, with the wife also becoming a Christian. These conversions are dramatic and easily remembered. In addition, *Links* sometimes recorded others also converted under Herbert's preaching. Maybe some did not persist in their new found faith. But clearly, others did. Herbert's ministry was a fruitful one.

ABRIDGE

Herbert was always looking for new ways of spreading the Gospel. He had developed a concern for people in the rural villages of Essex. Sometimes he cycled out to them and concluded that many of the isolated villagers were cut off from the Gospel. He prayed for guidance. Then he was offered, free of charge, a horse-drawn army engineer's wagon. He immediately saw its possibilities and altered it into a Gospel Wagon.

On July 10th, 1924, the wagon left South Woodford in the charge of Vic Jones and Roy Aylott, two students from the Bible Training Institute of Glasgow. Their first stopping place, just five and a half miles from Woodford, was Abridge, then a small village of about 300 people. Their arrival caused a stir for, apparently, not much happened in Abridge. The two missioners settled down to a programme of visiting homes and giving out tracts in the afternoons followed by a children's meeting and two open air services in the evening. One of the latter was next to the bus stop, so they often had a captive audience from the queue there. The two students were talented young men, with Vic possessing a fine tenor voice and Roy adept at playing the violin. Children were attracted to them and followed them around demanding more choruses. After the open airs, young men often came back to the wagon for further talks and about 30 professed conversion. The seeds of a permanent work had been sown.

The Gospel Wagon then rolled on to Ongar with two new missioners, Messrs Ellis and Sutton taking - literally - the reins. A pattern was established and every summer the wagon made its way around Essex visiting such places as Blackmore,

Sawbridgeworth and Fyfield. From 1927, a retired man, Mr Ted Smith, was able to give much time to the work. In 1931, particular success was recorded at Fyfield under two more young men, Messrs Rush and Cook. Throughout the twenties and thirties, many conversions were recorded with attempts to establish places of worship then often visited by Herbert.

The wagon's most long-lasting effect was at the very first place it visited, Abridge. Indeed, the impact was so strong that some people called it "revival". The revival provoked some opposition at first, and difficulties were met when the new converts sought a place to meet. After eight weeks in the Parish Room and four weeks in the local gym , gatherings had to be in a private house. Herbert, of course, prayed about the problem and a friend, who had dropped in to see him on another matter, offered £3-4000 towards a new building. The difficulty then was that no-one appeared willing to sell the land on which a church could be constructed save one farmer who put up an acre at the high price of £135. Herbert considered both the site and the price too large but the seller would reduce neither. Herbert delayed. Soon after, while attending church in Woodford, he heard the minister announce his text from Jeremiah 32 verse 9, "And I bought the field." The theme of the sermon was that the land was unimportant compared with the use to which it was put. Herbert went ahead. More money was donated and the Abridge Evangelical Church was opened on January 30th, 1926 with Herbert White as its pastor.

By 1928, the new church was running two church services and a children's meeting on Sundays, a prayer meeting on Tuesdays, a Women's Bright Hour on Wednesdays, and the Band of Hope on Thursdays. By 1930, Herbert noted that 16 adults had been baptised while in December of that year a special mission was conducted by a converted boxer, Charles Cutler.

One Abridge girl, Madeline, was 10 when the Gospel Wagon

first visited the village. A friend persuaded her to attend the Sunday School and she became a Christian at the age of 12. She was particularly helped by the Sunday School teacher whom she described as "the loving, gentle Miss Simmonds." It was the same Maud Simmonds who served as a sister at the Home and who every Sunday made her way to the village. Madeline records that children who did well in the scripture examinations sometimes joined those from the Home when Herbert took them to London. They would visit the bank where Herbert started work and where the manager provided cash for them all to have lunch in Lyons Corner House. Then followed a visit to a famous place like St Paul's Cathedral before listening to Herbert at Tower Hill. The conversion and teaching must have been sound for, over 60 years later, Madeline is still a strong Christian.

But it was not just Madeline. Her early home life had been unhappy with a drunken father and a mother who was also partial to drink. The local cobbler, who had started to attend the new Abridge Church, took them to hear Herbert there. Mother and father were converted and, with much support from Herbert, conquered their drink problems. Madeline adds that they were "transformed" with the father founding a successful business in supplying machinery for printers. The parents remained active members of the Abridge church for the rest of their lives.

Throughout the 1930's, the work at Abridge continued to grow. Herbert proved a capable pastor with his known strengths of preaching and arranging campaigns being supplemented by his developing skills in visiting and counselling people in spiritual need. He was now in his fifties and probably in his prime: the Home was well established with an increased number of children in property which the home owned: every Friday lunch-time, he preached at Tower Hill: his own family were growing up: and he was the pastor of an expanding church. The variety of his involvement, the range of his skills, and the continuance of his enthusiasm were remarkable.

The years of the Second World War brought change to Abridge. The Home moved to Tiptree where Herbert had to spend much of his time. A Mr Arnold Gilbert (who later married Olive White) was appointed co-pastor at the Abridge church. He proved an inspired choice. Possessed of an engaging, jolly personality, he not only kept the Sunday services going - even when enemy planes were droning overhead - he saw the possibility of something else. Several army and air force camps had been established nearby. The small villages were hardly centres of entertainment and the soldiers and airmen were often at a loose end. Mr Gilbert responded by turning the church hall into a canteen. Many villagers volunteered to help. With Olive White in charge of the small kitchen, the helpers peeled potatoes, prepared, cooked and served meals, sometimes to as many as 300 men per evening. Mr Gilbert acted as a genial host and the canteen became noted for its meals, recreation and friendly atmosphere. To obtain food for such numbers in war-time was a challenge in itself. One woman obtained permission to sow seeds in a local field and thereafter provided the luxury of fresh lettuces. Potatoes - chips were in constant demand - were often given just as at the Home in Woodford. Mr Gilbert somehow obtained supplies of fish and carried them to the hall by bus. People must have known when he was on board! In 1942, the bubbling Arnold was rejoicing that God provided a Christmas tree and 52 parcels for troops who had to spend Christmas Day away from their families.

Sundays posed a problem. The pastors did not want to sell goods on a Sunday, yet they did not want to deny the forces access to their favourite rendezvous. Their solution was to remain open and, to the amazement of the men, to give the refreshments free of charge. Mr Gilbert, in explaining the reasons, then had opportunities to witness to his faith.

Many troops were impressed by this practical Christianity and some began attending the church services. A number experienced conversions. Friendships were made and maintained even when the troops went abroad. Here are two extracts from letters to Mr Gilbert,

> "I felt there was something different from other canteens, the atmosphere was homely, the service was excellent, but I think what impressed me most was the cheerful sincerity of your helpers, so anxious to do all they could to make our few hours there as happy and as far removed from the barracks as possible. I would like to convey my personal thanks and undying gratitude to Miss White particularly for the superb excellence of the meals served under her expert supervision."
>
> "I will always remember the service in the little church, the sincerity and the simplicity which, to my mind, are the highest, purest ideals of Christianity. I consider myself privileged even to be associated with your church."

Mr Gilbert also told of the return of a soldier from fighting abroad. The man brought news of comrades who had attended the canteen and had now lost their lives, and greetings from those who had been wounded. These examples well convey the value of the Abridge outreach to the forces. The canteen provided a relaxed environment along with homely cooking - often so different from life at the camps. The church provided spiritual strength. Numbers of men turned to Mr Gilbert and his colleagues for advice and encouragement both with their personal family problems and with the prospect of facing death.

For all the attention given to the canteen, the church services were not neglected. On the contrary, participants from the village increased and a baptistery was built to cater for the adults baptised as a witness of their turning to God. The Sunday School and Boys' Brigade flourished. Money collected at the services so exceeded needs that a surplus was given to overseas missions. In July 1941, the Abridge Evangelical Church combined with the Church of England for an open air service which paved the way for united services held four times a year.

After the war, the canteen closed. The bustle, the steaming hot kitchen, the long lines of servicemen cheerfully waiting for meals, became but memories. The church continued to flourish. With the canteen shut, there was room to utilise the facilities for other purposes. Tuesday evenings were given over to three youth clubs of varying ages. Pastor Gilbert maintained his ministry until his sudden death in 1955, building links with many villagers and local organisations, conducting lively services, and finding time to visit the children at Woodford.

THE HOME

It is appropriate to come back to the Home for, in writing about Herbert's open air ministry, his preaching tours, his outreach to Abridge, there is a danger of overlooking the fact that he saw the Home as the main ground for evangelism. In 1901, in announcing the move to Crescent Road, the 23 year old Herbert indicated his intention also to hold a mission there. The following year he reported that seven people had been converted at the mission. Periodic missions followed, with services becoming more frequent following the opening of the Florence Barclay Hall. It was at such a mission, led by Captain Pinchbeck and his hand bell ringers, that Victor White felt the call of God. "I slipped down in my chair", Victor said when the challenge came, but soon after, "made a covenant with the Lord."

Above all, Herbert wanted the resident children to be won for Christ, an aim which was held just as strongly by Edith, Ma and other staff. The children were influenced through three main means. First, the daily prayers conducted, usually, by Herbert. "Prayers" meant also chorus singing, reciting Bible verses and a talk. Second, by Sunday School. Once the Florence Barclay Hall was available, Sunday School was held there although led by leaders coming in from the neighbourhood. Here much attention was given to study for

the Sunday School Union Scripture Examinations, a national
award which entailed the children gaining detailed knowledge
of Biblical passages. *Links* often reported the children's
successes in these examinations. The older children
continued to go to young people's meetings and services in
local churches. Third, by the lives of the staff. Of
course, at times, the Whites and the sisters did get annoyed
and short-tempered. Generally, however, the devotion,
cheerfulness, persistence and kindliness of the carers made
a deep impact on many of the children.

How effective was the Christian influence on the children?
It is impossible to quantify, difficult to judge. No doubt
some children were put off by Herbert's forceful style. No
doubt, some rejected Christianity. Such children are the
ones least likely to maintain contact with the Home and
hence I interviewed none of them. Peter Kemp recalled a
friend who "wasn't religious. He reacted against what he
was taught, but not against the Home." Some other children,
while not adopting the Home's evangelical Christianity, were
influenced by, and did appreciate its Christian ethical
standards.

Just as certainly, many of the children did become
Christians. Nothing gave Herbert White more delight than to
write, as he did in 1919,

> "We therefore greatly rejoice that many of our
> children have confessed Christ to be their Saviour
> and we had the unspeakable joy of baptising five
> of our old girls, one a married woman, in March
> last."

The annual report often contained similar statements which
rejoiced in children who had made decisions for Christ. But
decisions are one thing, maintaining them is another. Yet
clearly many of the converted children did continue their
faith into adulthood as evidenced by the many letters
published in *Links*. Some typical ones are as follows.

"It does not seem fifteen years ago since I first left the Home to earn my own living, and now I have a nice little home of my own, a good Christian husband and two little ones whom we want, with God's help, to train to be followers of Him who their mother learnt to love when she was a girl of twelve in that dear old Home in Woodford." (woman 1923)

"Although I failed when I first left the Home I shall never forget what I was taught when with you. I must tell you that I am now really converted and am trying to please the Lord day by day." (woman 1930)

"Since being in Norwich I have sometimes been to the Church of England service and hearing the Gospel in all its simplicity every time I went, continued to go. Well, a Sunday came during last year, it was a Missionary service and I just heard 'the voice' saying 'You have no one to leave - Go.' and that was all. From that time I have been seeking guidance regarding the Lord's will in the matter and shall hope one day, D.V., to take the Gospel Message to a Missionary Hospital... I shall never forget and always realise that it was at the Home where I first met Christ, who has just meant everything to me ever since, though often I fail Him." (woman, nurse, 1933)

"Would it be convenient for my young man and I to come over and see you. He is a good Christian worker and one I can be proud for you to meet. I want you to know that time spent on me during my seven years under your care was not in vain. We would be more than pleased if you could set aside a few minutes to pray for us and give us some advice along the pathway before us so that we may dedicate our lives anew to Christ our Saviour."

(woman, 1940)

"I still thank God for the day I was sent to you
for you to look after and bring up, as you have
done for many others for the past forty years and
I hope and pray that it will go on for another
like period." (man 1943)

"It was difficult to lead a consistent Christian
life but by the Grace of God I was able to
conquer, and once again I should like to give you
my thanks for the way we were all brought up in
the love of God... I should like to tell you some
of the things that happened to me spiritually
after I left the Home. After attending Church for
over a year, one evening God spoke to me very
definitely and it was then that I decided to
follow my Lord through the waters of baptism,
shortly after I took a Sunday School class and
when the season of open air meetings came around I
spoke on several different occasions and so by
these small services for the Lord my spiritual
life was greatly deepened." (man 1943)

"I often recall the evening prayers what you
conducted. How I loved to sing the choruses and
hymns with the other children. I remember, too,
your helpful talks and Bible Readings each day.
Please pray for me because I want the Lord to be
as close to me as He is to you. I am trying very
hard to keep a hold on what you and the sisters
taught me." (woman 1947)

The children were brought up in a Christian atmosphere where
many opportunities were presented for them to make an
individual commitment to Christ. Obviously the environment
was persuasive yet it was not forceful. None of the former
children whom I interviewed or communicated with by letter
complained of having religion forced down their throats.

Perhaps Jon Sweet is a good example with which to finish. A thoughtful boy, Jon spent long periods reflecting upon both his position in life as a child without parents and upon Christianity. As will be told in the next chapter, he spent some of his time in the Home at Tiptree but most at Woodford. He came to Christianity slowly and after consideration. He said,

> "It was in my time at Tiptree that I first made a commitment to the Lord. A Salvation Army couple came one evening to the front room in the Grove. I remember as a sign of my commitment that I went and tore up my American comics."

Jon's laugh about the comics underlies a significant point. Far from being gloomy, the Christianity at the Home always had a lighter touch. It was serious yet with a place for humour. As for Jon, he later moved back to urban Woodford which he found more irksome than the open spaces of the country. He continued,

> "I longed for the day when it would all end and I would be free. But my Christian commitment was deepening and, at the age of 14, I was baptised at Abridge."

After leaving the Home, Jon served an apprenticeship in engineering and subsequently became very active in church life.

One of the three objectives of the Home was "to be the means in God's hands of bringing children to know the Lord Jesus Christ as their personal Saviour." The letters in *Links,* the number of former residents who attended - and still attend - the annual gatherings, the many who maintain contact with the Home, are indicators that this aim was achieved with a large number of the children. Herbert and his colleagues were a powerful influence for Christianity amongst the young people for whom they cared.

Christian child care pioneers were a feature of the second half of the nineteenth and first half of the twentieth centuries. So too were strong Christian preachers with most towns having at least one minister noted for his ability to evangelise. What was unusual was for the two roles to be combined in one person. William Quarrier founded Quarrier's Homes and supported evangelical missions but, as his biographer notes, "He made no claim to be a preacher himself, but was able to bring to the city those who could gain the ear of the masses." [3] Charles Spurgeon was a preacher who drew thousands and who stimulated the development of Spurgeon's Homes but he never lived in the Homes. [4] Herbert White was unusual in that he combined both the capacity to run a children's home and also to preach the Gospel to many outside its doors.

Dr Martyn Lloyd-Jones declared that Herbert was "primarily an Evangelist concerned about bringing men and women and boys and girls to a knowledge of God through our Lord and Saviour Jesus Christ." [5] Probably Herbert himself would not have divided his life neatly into the two compartments of Home maker and evangelist. He and Ma founded the Home out of a concern for children which sprang from their Christian compassion. Thereafter the continuance of the work was a testimony to the power of God. In short, service and evangelism, works and faith, were both expressions of their Christianity.

References

1. D. Matisko (ed), *The Autobiography of George Muller,* Whitaker House, 1984, p.73.
2. *Links,* 1952, p.12.
3. A.Gammie, *William Quarrier,* Pickering & Inglis, 1937, p.40.
4. K.Triggs, *Charles Spurgeon,* Pickering Paperbacks, 1984.
5. *Links,* 1952, p.12.

V. Not Like Any Other Home 1939 - 1952

The Grove, Tiptree, had been purchased as a holiday centre. Judith Tell recalls Herbert telling her that he wished it was nearer the sea. She continued, "He didn't know that war was coming." In 1939, war was declared between Britain and Germany and soon London, including Crescent Road, was subjected to bombing. The children were already at Tiptree on holiday and so stayed on at the Grove. Otherwise they might have been scattered all over the country with the other evacuees. Once again, the Lord had prepared in advance and the majority moved to Tiptree in Essex.

TIPTREE

The Grove could accommodate about 60 children so ten or so had to be found lodgings. Herbert sought these out in what was the nearest he ever came to developing boarding-out. Most of the children had already enjoyed a holiday at the Grove and so welcomed the chance to settle in the country. It appeared ideal. A sprawling country house with out-buildings, a small lake, and acres of fields all set in the undulating Essex farmland famed for its fruit. Tiptree jam is still noted to this day. Yet, in some ways, the Grove presented difficulties for the staff. The rambling building was difficult to clean and almost impossible to heat. The cooking facilities were limited. The sleeping accommodation was insufficient with some of the boys initially having to bed down in the dining room. Water had to be boiled in a copper fired by wood. Bath time entailed a long time waiting for the water to be heated followed by the heavy work of transferring it into the tub and sink. For the staff, bath night could be an endurance test. And washing the clothes was not much easier.

Most enemy bombing was targeted on London, yet returning planes sometimes ditched their bombs on Essex. Consequently air-raid sirens went off in Tiptree as planes flew overhead.

After a while, the staff decided not to rouse the children although they still got up to patrol. Their long and tiring days were often followed by sleepless nights. Later in the war came the threat of the pilot-less V1's, the doodle-bugs as they were called. These would often fall short of London so the practice of getting children into the shelters had to be resumed. On one occasion, the children were inside the shelter during an attack. Herbert paced up and down outside as a V1 droned nearer. He was heard praying, "Lord, don't let my children get hurt." The rocket was shot down and crashed near by and a piece of shrapnel struck Herbert's tin helmet - without harming him.

With his own children grown up, Herbert probably spent more time in close contact with the children of the Home than ever before. Ewart White had been called up into the forces and was serving in Europe. Victor, now married to Margaret, embarked for India in 1941. Bunty joined the land-army. Olive remained at Woodford but devoted much of her time to Abridge. Edith still undertook much of the office work. And Ma, of course, still led, moulded and inspired what proved to be a magnificent team who were prepared to put up with all the difficulties. Sisters Gladys (who married Herbert junior), Jean Morrow (who married Ewart), Eileen Harris, Mary Runnacres, Winifred Caplin, Lily Evans and Ann Hammond are now names to be read in the annual reports. To the children they were everyday companions, carers, and parent figures. They emerged as a loyal and stable group and, at the end of the war, Herbert rightly and publicly voiced "A thousand thanks to our sisters who have so splendidly laboured in the work for some years and have kept together during the difficult war years." Praise indeed from Herbert. In addition, Herbert junior, who was not conscripted, gradually took over responsibility for "outside duties". In 1944, he and his wife, Gladys, moved into a bungalow provided by yet another friend and headed up the Grove farm. The 20 acres, farmed by Herbert, two volunteers, and a boy, produced milk, vegetables, fruit, poultry, and eggs. Much went into the Home for consumption, but the surplus was sold and brought in the sizeable sum of £500 a year.

Even before the farm was fully developed, the Home continued to experience God's provision. The beginning of war had brought an end to the regular supply of fish. It also meant the introduction of food rationing. Yet in 1940 Herbert was praising God for the gifts of eggs, rabbits, hares, pheasants, bacon, jam and fruit. Simultaneously, faced also with a clothing shortage, Herbert received a visit from a friend who promptly measured all the children and later returned with new suits, coats, shirts and dresses for them all. By August of that year, however, the Home faced a financial crisis being down to the last shilling. Herbert prayed. The weekend went by with no gifts arriving. On the Monday, the post brought six letters but no money. Herbert recorded,

> "I sat down in my chair and said, 'what does this mean, Lord?' Later on someone rung me up from about thirty miles away, and he said, 'I cannot tell you all the details but you will hear of something to your benefit before the week is out.' On the Thursday in that week I received a letter from a man in Bermondsey whom I had never seen, or his family, and in his letter he said, 'In accordance with the wish frequently expressed by my mother, I have great pleasure in making a gift from her estate of £500.'"

And so it went on. As always the yearly income was sufficient. For 1942-43, the expenses of £2531 were met by an income of £3237. Given the absence of many people in the forces and the shortages caused by the war, such income was amazing.

It was not just money. In 1942, Herbert received a phone call saying, "There is a cow on the way full of new milk. It will be at your place in half an hour. Please see that it is milked as soon as it arrives." Herbert did not say if he had ever milked a cow before. But, at a time of milk scarcity, it proved a welcome addition. Once the farm was under way, the heavy pulling created a need for a horse. Almost to order, a man drove up in a large wagon and announced, "I have got a mare for you."

The children loved the animals. The staff were more appreciative of a new bathroom for which much prayer had been made. Gifts arrived sufficient not just for a bathroom but also a laundry. The next difficulty was that permission to build - not easy to obtain in war-time - had to be secured. After more prayer, the green light was given and the staff could wash both bodies and clothes in comfort.

Herbert even got his rice. Yes, rice. He was very partial to rice pudding which he justified on the grounds of being part of a healthy diet. Rice was extremely scarce but Herbert prayed. One morning a phone call came from a puzzled customs officer at Liverpool to say that a large consignment of rice from Peru had arrived for the Home. Herbert too was puzzled for he knew no-one in Peru. He explained to the astonished official that God must have sent it. The officer coped by granting permission for the rice to be forwarded on condition that some was given to the local hospital - a condition which Herbert gladly met.

Herbert enjoyed Tiptree. Perhaps it was his increasing age - now in his sixties - perhaps the war-time restrictions on travel, but for some reason he began to relax. The rule about keeping quiet during meals was abolished. Children were allowed to roam around the extensive grounds. Judith Tell records that the girls who knew him at Tiptree spoke not about his discipline but "how kind and loving he was." Peter Kemp explained how he got close to Herbert there,

> "As a young child I saw him from a distance. At
> Tiptree I started to work on the farm while most
> of the others were still at school. As the

eldest boy I came into contact with him. He expected me to discipline the younger children. He would say, 'Peter, I understand the boys have been scrumping apples. Do something about it.' So he was talking to me and he used to take me with him when he preached at local churches. He would tell me all that the Lord was doing in his work, how he wanted to get back to Woodford etc. I didn't talk to him as much as listen. But it was not restrictive."

Unlike Peter, Jon Sweet came as a younger child to Tiptree. He explains,

"I was conceived during the war. My mother's husband was away fighting and she had a liaison. When I was born she signed adoption papers and left me in a nursing home. My father collected me and placed me in the care of a girl friend who in turn passed me to another couple to be looked after. When the war ended my father took me to live in the same house as his girl friend and new wife and family. I became delinquent and it was decided that I should be placed in care. The lady who had cared for me as a baby knew of the Children's Home and Mission and was able to influence the decision to send me there when I was ten years old. She was a Christian who later became my adoptive mother. I remember Herbert, quite a heavily built man, very caring. I stayed in Woodford just one night then I got into Herbert's renowned Hillman and he took me to Tiptree.

I had 15 months at Tiptree. For a lot of my childhood I had been constrained. An elderly couple had kept me in the bedroom a lot of the time. So Tiptree with its lovely grounds, farm conditions, lots of space, places to muck around, to hide, build dens, was a paradise for a boy who had been constrained.

We walked to school, a mile and a half, through the strawberry fields. I was a bit of a dreamer. I had switched off. I did not make much of relationships with people - Miss Harris was the member of staff I got on best with. But I thoroughly enjoyed it, lots of kids to play with. I loved it.

The dormitory used to be the stable so there was a long line of iron framed beds, about 15 of us, polished wooden floor. The girls were in the main house, the Grove. There was a main hall with a stage in it and a big. coke-burning stove which we used to gather round in the evenings.

There was a pond and we had an old water tank which we rowed - and capsized. We went on an outing to Clacton and went through the Tunnel of Love. That set us building ghost houses in the out-buildings into which we beguiled people."

The enjoyable experiences described by Jon Sweet explain why the Homes children, in general, welcomed the move to Tiptree. But their arrival initially was not welcomed by all local residents. They almost doubled the population of the Tiptree school so causing crowded classrooms for the pupils and time tabling problems for the teachers. The outcome was some conflict, with the local children chanting,

"Here comes the Grove,
All dressed in mauve,
Living on charity,
Huddling round a stove."

In an outburst of anger, one teacher called them "Grove

scroungers", a nickname that stuck.[1] Slowly the animosity
lessened and by Jon's time had almost disappeared. None the
less, it deeply hurt some of the Home's children.

The school experiences apart, former children cite nothing
but happy memories of Tiptree. The local Congregational
Church welcomed the new arrivals, and invited Herbert to
preach. Much mention is also made of the Christmases at
Tiptree with the Woodford tradition of carols, many games,
fun, and ample food being continued. One change was that
the Christmases had the extra presence of soldiers. The
padre at the R.A.M.C. barracks at nearby Kelvedon had known
Herbert at Woodford and happened to tell his fellow officers
- most of whom were doctors - about the Home and the faith
on which it was built. Some of the officers determined to
see for themselves and, in particular, wanted to see a cow
which had been provided by prayer. They visited and were so
impressed by the staff and children that they joined in the
festivities of Christmas 1942 with the Colonel performing as
Father Christmas. The children loved having the soldiers
around and, interestingly, the latter were moved by the
lives of some of the children. A number began to attend
church and the padre, Hugh McCullough, later recorded,

> "It was lovely to bring some of my soldiers there.
> It was still more lovely to see those children and
> to hear them sing their praise to God. I have
> seen tears in the eyes of strong, stalwart
> soldiers because memories had been awakened
> through the simple testimony given by these lads
> and lasses."[2]

Delightful as Tiptree was in the summer, the children still
enjoyed outings to the sea side. In 1946 they went to
Walton-on-Naze and, when they returned, yet another friend
of the Home was there. Observing their happiness and
appreciation, he immediately said, "Arrange another outing
and send me the account." So the following week they all
went to Dovercourt. That year they even had a trip to

Woodford.

Tiptree, for all its memories of sun, fruit and fields, was clouded by one event. On February 6th, 1942, Ma Hutchin died.

Ma's retiring, self-effacing nature probably hid many of her talents. She must have been a superb organiser and manager of people. For over 40 years, she ensured that a Home, caring for up to 80 children at any one time, ran like clockwork. Within it, she co-ordinated a term of self-sacrificing, lowly paid workers who functioned with few of the divisions and conflicts which can characterise institutions. This apart, four features about Ma stand out.

First was her loving dignity. Herbert White put it, "She had a bearing about her that led to respect." In the midst of feeding and getting scores of children ready for school, she retained a calmness. Despite her small stature, she had few problems in keeping discipline and control. Children loved her.

Second was her sheer hard work. From early morning for 42 years, Ma was at work. She personally cooked, made clothes, mended shoes, cut hair, decorated rooms. More, she passed these skills on to the other staff and children. Then, in the evening, she would gather half a dozen children around the fire in her room to darn socks, to enjoy a sweet and listen to her Bible stories. The affection associated with that room stayed in the memories of many children. Precious times.

Third was her devotion to individual children, particularly those who were sick or troubled. One former child recalled that, when she was ill,

> "Ma slept every night at the foot of the bed and I had a fire night and day. Getting up to tend to

me and sitting with me during the day when she thought I was lonely... when I look back I can see such a lot of little things which showed how much she cared about us all and I wish I had thanked her at the time, but there can't be many who live in so many hearts... Truly she was a Mother to us all."[3]

Fourth was her Christian faith, as firm and enduring as Herbert's. As Victor White said, "She gave her life first to God and then to the family - and it was non stop, seven days a week." Ma did not seek public notice but she was sometimes prevailed upon to speak at the annual meetings. In 1931 it was recorded that she "Very diffidently rose to speak but her voice soon took on a note of enthusiasm." She thanked all those who supported the Home and added, "We do not go to the world, we do not go to God's people. God Himself does that. We go to God and He picks out one here and there, and so our needs are met." Ma's faith was quiet yet strong. All who knew her knew of her trust in God.

Herbert, her friend and fellow-founder, conducted the funeral service. Her gravestone at the Tiptree church bears the simple yet profound inscription, "She mothered 600 children." Some years later, Victor White tells of a former boy, by then in his seventies, who came back after an absence of many years. He sought out Ma's grave then "pulled away from his wife and said, 'Ma, I've always wanted to do this. Thank you.'"

A NEW BRITAIN

During the time the Home was based at Tiptree, Britain was undergoing radical social changes. Obviously the war resulted in family separations, the blitz, destruction, death to civilians and combatants and, finally, victory. Yet the same war also sparked off reforms to Britain's welfare system.

The war-time coalition government, sensing a need to build a better society for the ordinary citizens who were fighting the war, appointed William Beveridge to chair a committee to inquire into social insurance. His famous *Report on Social Insurance and Allied Services* (1942) contained detailed proposals to attack the giants of "Want, Disease, Ignorance, Squalor and Idleness." The coalition government agreed on the Education Act (1944) which ensured free secondary education for all and the Family Allowances Act (1945) which provided allowances paid directly to mothers. But the Conservative leader, Winston Churchill, incidentally the M.P. for Woodford, was wary of other Beveridge proposals which were accepted enthusiastically by the Labour Party. The outcome was a landslide victory for the latter in the general election of 1945 and there followed the National Health Service Act (1946), the National Insurance Act (1946), and the National Assistance Act (1948). They were accompanied by a massive housing drive and rising employment. The effects were profound. The 1948 Act contained the words, "The existing poor law shall cease to have effect." The workhouse really was abolished. Working class families benefited by allowances for their children, a free health service soon to be the envy of the world, unemployment pay given for a certain period without a means test, national assistance for the destitute and the possibility of decent housing. Just as important, unemployment became negligible. At last, effective steps had been taken against the gross material hardship, the extensive homelessness, the lack of medical treatment, and the near starvation which had characterised the lives of the poorest in the first half of the century. In the long run, these reforms were to alleviate the sheer physical want and suffering which had forced many parents to give up their children to public and voluntary bodies.

The case for welfare reform had also been backed from an unexpected quarter - evacuation. During the war, over three million children, the present writer among them, had been taken from their urban homes and transported to the safety of the country. The social historian, Arthur Marwick, concluded that this mass movement of mainly working class children, "brought to middle and upper-class households a consciousness for the first time of the deplorable conditions endemic in the rookeries and warrens which still existed in Britain's greatest industrial cities, and so, among the articulate few, aroused a new sense of social concern." [4] The pressure of this few then contributed to the pressure for the welfare legislation of the late 1940s.

The evacuation also stimulated interest in the difficulties of children separated from their parents. Officials began to realise that the existing child welfare services probably could not cope with the anticipated numbers of children made homeless or orphans by the war. Simultaneously, influential women, particularly Lady Allen of Hurtwood, developed a concern for the day care of children whose mothers were working in the war effort. Lady Allen's interest broadened to children in residential institutions and she and her colleagues pushed the government into establishing committees - chaired by Myra Curtis for England and Wales and James Clyde for Scotland - to consider the care of children deprived of a normal home life. The committees made extensive examinations of existing statutory and voluntary agencies. They investigated especially voluntary homes which were looking after 33,500 children in England and Wales and 4,788 in Scotland. Members of the Curtis Committee personally visited 140 voluntary homes. Their findings will be returned to in the next chapter. Here it is sufficient to outline the main recommendations of the two reports, namely

> that the responsibility for deprived children should be with one not several central government departments: that within local authorities a new department should be created with sole oversight of such children: that the preferred methods for the care of children away from their own families were, in order, adoption, fostering, residential care:

that where residential care was necessary it should be in small homes run by trained staff:

that voluntary organisations should continue to play a full part in the care of children although subject to close statutory inspection.

These recommendations were then incorporated into the Children Act (1948) with the Home Office becoming the responsible government department and the new local authority service being named Children's Departments.

BACK TO WOODFORD

These changes were eventually to have implications for the Home and, indeed, for all voluntary child care bodies. But, while the new legislation was coming into being, the Home was gradually returning to Woodford. After the war, bomb damage in Crescent Road made an immediate move back impossible. On his demob from the forces, Ewart White and his wife, Jean, together with Victor and Margaret oversaw the repairs and re-equipping of the Woodford premises. Progress was slow due to a national shortage of materials and a long and terrible winter in 1946-47. But early in 1947, 21 children went from Tiptree to Woodford to join 12 girls taken in from the Mount Hermon Girls Orphan Home in Sevenoaks which had had to close.

For a while, 27 children remained at Tiptree with Ewart and Jean now transferring to be in charge there assisted by sisters Dorothy and Eileen. Jon Sweet, who stayed there during this period, remembered, "Mrs Ewart White was the lady of the house. Herbert White junior and his wife ran the farm and we went to collect the milk in a churn. Herbert was never brought to prominence. He was ordinary. We loved him. He used to let kids get on the horse then he'd whack it." Herbert junior had suffered some kind of breakdown from which he never fully recovered. By 1951, Mrs Jean White felt unable to continue so she and Ewart withdrew. The remaining youngsters were then taken back to

Woodford. By 1952, the Grove was back to its original purpose as a holiday and convalescent centre under a Mr and Mrs Schwier, farmers from Bedford, who offered their services just at the right time.

Meanwhile, in the late 1940s, the Home at Woodford was experiencing such a pressure for its places that it had a waiting list. The Children Act (1948) with its expected expansion of both local authority work and fostering had still to be implemented. The war had meant the separation of many husbands and wives resulting, in some cases, in the break-up of marriages and the birth of children outside of wedlock. Not least, the reputation of the Home seemed to be growing amongst officials so that an increasing number of applications came from probation officers, health visitors and N.S.P.C.C. inspectors. Some typical cases were as follows.

A father returned from a P.O.W. camp to find his wife in a mental hospital, his home gone, and his two children with their grandparents whose care was not adequate. The father obtained a job and arranged for the children to enter the Home.

A mother was left with six children when her husband deserted. She could not cope with the youngest who appeared under-nourished. An official from the local Council of Social Service arranged a meeting between the mother and the Home with the result that the four year old girl - younger than most who entered - was accepted.

A widow died leaving two children. A friend took them in for a while but found difficulties with the 11 year old "highly strung, under weight boy". An officer from the Family Welfare Association arranged for the Home to take him.

During the war, a boy was the sole survivor of a bomb

which killed his mother and grand-parents. He was then evacuated until his father returned from the forces. The father re-married but this soon broke-up. The lone father could not manage his son and a District Care Organiser found a place for the ten year old in the Home.

Before long, Woodford alone contained over 60 children. The pressure of children revealed two staffing needs. One concerned the need for more workers to come and live within the Home. Nationally there was a shortage of staff for residential work. Jack Mitchell in his autobiography tells how, without any previous experience or qualifications, he obtained in 1945 the post of assistant superintendent in a local authority children's home of 100 children.[5] In the understaffed home, he soon tired and eventually had to withdraw. The odds must have seemed against the Home in Woodford obtaining more staff particularly as it refused to advertise for them and gave no promises about salary. Yet in 1947 five new workers offered their services. Before long, Woodford had nine and Tiptree six staff members. The other need concerned the leadership of the Home. Herbert and Edith were approaching their seventies and were finding it more difficult to deal with the increased administration and more complex relationships with statutory bodies. Herbert became convinced that his youngest son, Victor, should take over. But Victor was still serving in the army in India. Eventually Herbert wrote to his son revealing his thoughts. Meanwhile Margaret White, Victor's wife, who had stayed working in the Town Clerk's Department of a local authority, also felt that Victor's place was in the Home but did not want to influence him. At last she wrote to tell him her thoughts. Victor, who had all along envisaged a career in the City, was praying about his future and finally wrote to tell Margaret that he believed the Lord was telling him to work in the Home. Amazingly, all three letters crossed in the post. Accordingly, when Victor did return, he and Margaret threw in their lot with the Home. In 1947, Herbert made it clear that Victor should succeed him as director.

The position in the post-war years was thus of Victor gradually taking over from his father. In many ways, life was similar to that before the war. Friends continued to give their support. Dr. Flegg, long retired but still in touch, died in March, 1947. Dr. Eric Mathie returned from service abroad and with Dr David Smith and Dr Carey Baker resumed the medical service. Mr Stephen Smith acted as dentist and A.C. Thompson as chiropodist. The Seven Kings Sewing Group finally ended in 1943 and Mr Suckling of the Boot Fund died in the same year. But eight groups, now called Working Parties were thriving by 1950 along with the Shroeburyness Boot Fund. Most importantly, the faith in and dependence upon God were the same. And God was the same. In 1949, Herbert was rejoicing that the Hillman had completed 80,000 miles and was still going strong. He stated in his annual report,

> "What thrills us so is the truly marvellous way in
> which God knows and meets the need of the moment.
> A few months back, we found we were in need of
> cups for the children, and when we were wondering
> what to do, some friends called bringing parcels
> which included 50 cups!
> Another time we were especially requiring socks
> and a friend wrote saying that she felt she had to
> send some along."

Herbert never asked anyone except God for a penny and the Home never went into debt. Income continued to rise to meet costs. Its sources, though, were often different from the early days. In 1950-51, the £7049-13s-10d received included £3094-14s-4d from legacies and £1054-6s-6d as payments for children from parents and statutory bodies.

Much was the same yet important changes could be discerned. Three stand out. First, more children appeared to be returning to their parents. Herbert was always ahead of his time in recognising that children removed from the physical care of parents still retained emotional bonds with them. His thinking was shaped more by the Christian emphasis on the importance of the natural family than on psychological concepts about the imprinting of such bonds. But, whatever the reason, he had never set barriers between children in the Home and their parents. By the 1950s, official child care policy was on the same lines. The extra ingredient was that the welfare reforms, coupled with full employment, meant that more parents could now provide materially for their families. In 1950-51, 18 children left the Home - an unusually high number - with 13 going back to their parents.

Secondly, as the quality of life improved for most working class children in Britain so it did for those in the Home. The number of outings and other activities increased. In 1947, the children enjoyed six excursions to the seaside. The following year, they also had six parties laid on by nearby churches plus visits to such places as the Kensington and British Museums, London Zoo and the Tower of London. In 1951, most of the children holidayed at Tiptree for three weeks. While there, a number of trips were made in a double decker bus to the seaside where they could now spend their weekly pocket money. Sporting events against local teams were a regular feature and the present writer played cricket for the South Ilford Covenanters against the Home. The Covenanters lost. Education horizons broadened. Educational reforms meant that fees did not have to be paid for staying on at grammar school and more of the Home's children were passing the 11 plus examination and going to the county high and grammar schools.

Thirdly, the Home was now subject to the Children Act (1948). At the annual meeting of 1948, the chairman, James Stokes, one of the trustees, welcomed the act as "A great humanitarian measure for looking after young people in our land" but warned that it was "going to make great demands on a work like this." He was referring to the new

regulations laid upon voluntary homes and the fact that they
would be subject to more regular and careful inspection from
the Home Office. One of those early inspectors was Robert
Tod whom the present writer was able to interview in 1992.
Mr Tod's own background was a conventional middle class one,
much of which has been spent in the civil service. On
visiting the Home, his initial reaction was that,

> "It hadn't been inspected for a long time. I got
> a very extra-ordinary impression. It was not like
> any other home. They were very strict, rather
> poor, very friendly, more religious than other
> Homes. The standard of care was modest but not
> poverty-stricken. There were about 60 children.
> They had their own religion. They went through the
> whole Bible. They went by the faith principle.
> It seemed to work.
> When I went a second time, it was with notice.
> The children were reasonably dressed, not smart,
> not shabby."

Mr Tod, who made one or two inspections a year, suggested
that the children be broken down into smaller groups in
order to create more of a family feeling. He was pleased
when this happened. He also called one summer and took
pleasure in watching the children play in tents they had
made for themselves.

Robert Tod seemed wryly amused that anyone could rely on
faith to feed 60 children. But, as he said, the important
fact was that,

> "The children were happy. There was a happy
> atmosphere. There was affection between staff and
> children. They had great respect for Herbert
> White. I don't think they had any qualifications
> but we didn't make a fuss about that then. None
> of them were rigid. Perhaps some were
> unimaginative."

Once the inspector went to the annual meeting, Our Day. He enthused over the children's choir, saying,

"My word, the singing was terrific. I thought to myself, if they sing like this, they are giving something to the children. It was not like any other Home at all."

The Home Office inspector's views give an unusual but generally favourable evaluation of the Home. Hopefully it contributes to one of the aims of this book which has been to present an accurate picture of what life in the Home was like. As far as possible the study has used the opinions of people who were actually in the Home and particularly of former children. It is fitting therefore to give one more account of a typical day near the end of Herbert's life. It is by Jon Sweet,

"We got up about 7.30am. Victor White used to come round and put on the lights. He did it very nicely but you got up. There were about a dozen in the dormitory and you queued up to get washed. Some poor kids were so strung up that they wet their beds so they had to clean up first. We had certain jobs to do like cleaning the stairs, washing the hand-basins, sweeping the playground. Then to breakfast. In those days, the bottom hall was open plan, round the outside were the lockers and we all had one. Breakfast was served on half a dozen scrubbed tables. We would stand by our chairs until grace was said then we would have breakfast. The meals were plain but wholesome - plenty of cereal and bread. During harvest times, food came in bulk - fruit, lots of marrows, harvest loaves.

I went to St Barnabas Secondary Modern School. We didn't have to walk together. I didn't do well. I switched off, I was a dreamer. I used to be

imaginative and quite good at English and wrote in
the school magazine. There were also children in
the school from Barnardo's. One day I got into a
terrific fight with one of their boys. He was
huge and pummelled me. If you upset anybody it
came out, 'You're only a Homes kid.' But I must
not overstate that.

We came home for dinner, then back to school.
Home once more, we changed our clothes. We might
have a little bit of homework. It was a bread and
butter world, not so much interest in education
then. People looked after us, kept us clean and
well fed - and that was good. Today we would
expect a lot more. There might be some more jobs
to do before tea. We played football and cricket,
mainly within the confines of the Home but
gradually doing more outside in clubs and the
Boys' Brigade.

Prayers came after tea. Sometimes these were
taken by Mr Gilbert which was a rare treat. He
was a Father Christmas of a man, big, white
haired, wing collar, bow tie. He was the Pastor
at Abridge but must have worked in the City. You
listened to him. He baptised me. There was a
strict regime at bed-time and you earned your
right to stay up."

"A VICTORIOUS END"

November 20th, 1949 marked the 50th anniversary of the
Children's Home and Mission. On Saturday 19th, former
children gathered in the Florence Barclay Memorial Hall and
the celebrations included what Herbert called "a riotous
hour" of games. On the 20th itself, two of the girls from
the Home were baptised at the Evangelical Free Church in
Abridge. The combination of unity, fun and public witness
fittingly reflected much of the previous half a century.

Soon after, Herbert's health began to deteriorate and by the autumn of 1951 it was obvious that he had terminal cancer. His last illness was borne bravely both by Herbert and by Edith.

Jon Sweet recalls the Christmas of 1951. The children enjoyed the usual carols, games, plenty of food and bags of excitement. A typical Home Christmas. Then on Christmas Day they gathered in the Florence Barclay Hall and Jon stated,

> "They rigged up a public amplification system from number 10 to the hall and I remember Herbert speaking to us. It was a bit like the king speaking and we all sat and listened with awe."

Herbert, from his sick bed, conveyed the Christmas story and his last words were,

> "I want to appeal to you all to accept Him that you might have the joy and strength of the Lord Jesus, taking you through life to a victorious end. God bless you. I shall be praying for you all the time."

The system was then left on so that Herbert could enjoy listening to the children at the games.

Herbert White died in March, 1952. His body was carried into the church by six of the young men. Fittingly, the church was full of those who had been at the Home as children, staff and friends. The service, it was recorded in *Links*, was not like a funeral service as it was characterised by "a note of praise and of victory." His life had, indeed, come to "a victorious end." The service to mark that end finished with one of his favourite hymns, "Guide me O thou great Jehovah."

Not Like Any Other Home

References

1. K. White, *A Place for Us,* Mill Grove, 1976,p.75.
2. *Links,* November, 1946,p.6.
3. *Links,* 1993,p.16
4. A. Marwick, *The Home Front,* Thames & Hudson, 1976,p.75.
5. E.J.Mitchell, *A Cornishman Remembers,* Campaign Literature, 1991, p.53.

Gospel Wagon at Fyfield, 1931

Ma Hutchin in later years

The Grove, Tiptree

An outing from Abridge. Mr Gilbert is on the left and Herbert White on the right

Herbert and Edith White - perhaps the last photo of them together

Victor and Margaret White, 1982

Children enjoying a meal, 1952

Herbert White greets an 'old girl' at the Golden Jubilee

VI. Herbert White

Certain facts about Herbert White's life brook no argument. Between 1899-1952, the home which he founded with Ma Hutchin cared for over 800 children. In that period, it received over £100,000 without any public appeal. There is no doubt, too, that Herbert White made a great impact on many people. In 1935, the Rev. D. Moore exclaimed, "He is the liveliest man I know. He is alive from top to bottom." Mr Robert Carnegie, added in the same year, "What a happy face he has. It is always beaming with joy." His daughter, Olive, who was close to him for many years, simply said, he was "dynamic." Dr. Martin Lloyd-Jones said of him,

> "I like always to meet a great man and to listen to a great man and I was one of those who was in a sense thus a hero-worshipper of our friend Mr Herbert White."[1]

Herbert thus received the highest praise from the leading evangelical figure of his time.

The danger in writing a biography of a great man is to present him as a straightforward almost perfect saint. But this was not Herbert. From what is known about him, it is clear that his personality contained paradoxical, even conflicting, features. To give a true picture of the man, five of these must be outlined.

First, *prominent/retiring*. Herbert stood out in a crowd. When a train stopped in a tunnel, Herbert broke out in a hymn and then preached. He thrived at gathering an audience around him in the open air. At times, he would march around the Home expecting staff and children to attend to any fault he spotted. As Judith Tell said, "He really enjoyed the special occasion - when he went on an excursion he was a completely different person. At Guy Fawkes night we used to have a massive bonfire. Mr White used to set off nearly all the fireworks. He loved it. We had the sparklers." Herbert bounced around at Christmas time, fostering enthusiasm and organising games. He also made much of the annual gathering, Our Day. Doreen Summer, who was in the Home during the 1940s and 50s, recalled that Herbert fussed around and "everyone and everything had to be just perfect. I remember we all had to stand as if we were in a choir in the church where we had to sing and then recite the scriptures. We were a bit afraid that we would make a mistake and one couldn't help but notice the expression on his face. It was one of pleasure and expectation, and at the end of his speech he seemed to be very happy and proud of us all."

Yet the same man also possessed a modest and retiring side. He never took up the suggestions that he should write a book or have one written about himself. He never sought publicity in the local, national or religious media. He refused to allow the Home to be called White's Homes. One local vicar came to Our Day and admitted that he had only recently heard about the work although he had lived in the area for nine and a half years.

Second *trust/anxiety*. Herbert's life was built upon trust in God. Other Christians were astonished at his lack of worry and complete confidence in God's provision when the Home was without food or money. One minister recalls driving with Herbert and recounted, "Suddenly he said, 'Praise the Lord' and slapped his hands on his two knees and said, 'Brother, I have not a care in the world'." Yet at that time he had around 80 children to look after. At times, however, his anxieties did weigh heavily upon him. He could become low in spirit and once suffered some kind of breakdown.

Third, *Victorian/modern*. Jon Sweet stated, "Herbert was one of those strong individuals thrown up by the conditions and attitudes of the end of the last century - strong, determined, people of great character. He knew his mind,

had deep convictions, a powerful figure." Herbert was bred in Victorian times and, in some ways, carried nineteenth century attitudes well into the next century. He bears comparison with other Victorian child care pioneers. Like Rudolf, he got things done. Like Barnardo, he carried a presence which made others stand in awe of him. Doreen Summer, who was mainly at Woodford while Herbert concentrated on Tiptree, commented on a visit from Herbert, "Everything and everyone was made ready before he arrived, as if royalty was expected, as if for inspection... When he was on the scene at times there was a hush around the room." Like Quarrier, he was hardly democratic in his practice. Alexander Gammie says of Quarrier, "There was something of the autocrat about him... No committee could hamper him." [2] Autocrat is too strong a word for Herbert for he certainly prayed with and listened to his family, colleagues and trustees. But he was the one who made the final decision. He was the one who decided which children were admitted. Further, just as a Victorian mill-owner assumed that power would pass on to his family so Herbert seemed to take it for granted that the directorship of the Home and many positions within it should be with the White family. Sometimes, too, his Victorian, paternalistic manner even infuriated his children - although they did not show it. Olive recounts, "He would always open the post at breakfast and leave the envelopes on the floor. Then he'd take the letters back to the office and leave the envelopes there for us to pick up." Again, like a number of Victorian evangelicals, Herbert could over-generalise about social problems. Thus in 1947, he gave his support to the view "that two thirds of the juvenile crime today is the result of the cinema." Even his clothing was rather Victorian with his inevitable suits, pin striped black trousers, and boots.

Yet for all his old fashioned dress, Herbert did not always retain Victorian beliefs and practices. He soon rejected the typical Victorian condemnation of parents who could not look after their own children. He saw the limitations of the gaunt, large, institutions which so many Victorians saw as suitable for orphan children. He displayed little of the Victorian love for pomp, position and hierarchy. The large voluntary children's societies often vied with each other to gain the approval and presence of V.I.P.s, aristocrats, even royalty. Not so Herbert. Nobody was invited to the annual meeting or to join the trustees just because of their social standing. No member of the royalty or aristocracy became a patron. Herbert had something of the radical leveller about him. He felt at home with the working class pastor of an east end mission, a clerk in a railway carriage, a private soldier in the barracks. He never sought honours or titles for himself. Herbert may have been a Victorian in the twentieth century but he was also a modern in Victorian clothing.

Fourth, *impulsiveness/patience.* Herbert's character contained a fiery, impulsive, streak. Peter Kemp recalls him driving off and making the football team walk home after they put up a poor display. Judith Tell received a sudden, sharp slap around the face when she made a cheeky reply. As his grandson, Keith White, put it, he could be "completely unpredictable." For instance, he liked meal-times to go like clockwork with everything arranged in advance, everyone on time and in their correct places. Yet sometimes he would upset the whole routine by charging in with several guests without any warning. Occasionally, he would blurt out an idea as though it would happen. In 1914, he announced that the Home would be split into two with the girls going to a seaside location. On reflection, he perceived the disadvantages and abandoned the proposal.

On the other hand, Herbert possessed tremendous patience. He wanted security of tenure for the houses in Crescent Road yet for years he turned aside suggestions - even from the landlord - that he take out a mortgage on them. He was prepared to wait until God moved a man to buy the freehold. Again, much as the Home needed a large hall, he would not allow the building to commence until he was sure it was the right course. One other example of his patience, or long-suffering, came from a number of former children who were interviewed. Jon Sweet, for instance, pointed out that although the Home has several difficult children, there were "no youngsters that I knew of that they had to shift because they couldn't cope with them." Judith Tell considered that the only misdeed likely to endanger a child staying was bullying so extreme as to make life unbearable for others. Herbert never reacted quickly to get rid of naughty children. He may have been impulsive over some issues but he was patient over the long-term interests of the Home and its residents.

Fifth, *independence/dependence*. All human beings are a mixture of independence and dependence. Indeed, an emotionally healthy person is one who can accept and incorporate both elements. Herbert White was unusual in that both traits were very prominent in his personality.

His independence is more obvious, He had a vision about starting a Home and, once convinced it was God's calling, nothing could stop him. Against the advice of his bank colleagues, some friends, and his in-laws, he gave up his safe position at the bank. He even tells with relish how a Christian minister was horrified that he should launch out on his own. But Herbert was quite prepared to be independent of employers and ministers. He thrived on the responsibilities laid upon him first as leader of the Home and later as pastor of the Abridge church. In this respect the comments of two people have particular weight. Jon Sweet became a Christian minister and then the holder of an important office in a Christian organisation. Keith White was not only Herbert's grandson but later became prominent as a writer, lecturer and facilitator of community agencies. Both said it was difficult to imagine Herbert "fitting in" with the other organisations, difficult to see him giving much time to committees or working under others. Herbert White certainly possessed a strong streak of independence.

Simultaneously, Herbert was very dependent upon two women.

His wife Edith was essential to his ability to cope. Keith White states that "She and Herbert were perfectly matched. His bustle was balanced by her quietness; his impetuosity by her serenity; his daring and imagination by her willingness to back him up in whatever he did." [3] This does not mean that Edith was the weaker of the two. Herbert depended upon her for the love and approval which reinforced his conviction that his actions were right. He depended upon her to provide the bulk of the day to day caring and discipline of their own children: the six White children did often miss their dad at meal times: they did resent that sometimes he was unable to be with them on their birthdays: they did question why he had to spend so much time with other people's children: this situation contained the seeds of family discord: it is much to Edith's credit that she could explain to the children the reasons for their unusual life-style and - in combination with the love she gave to them - explain in such a way that family unity was maintained. Not least, Herbert depended upon Edith for emotional and physical nursing at times of crises as when Herbert junior was injured, when Eunice died, when Herbert himself was spent and exhausted. If Edith had died young then it is difficult to see how Herbert could have coped.

The other woman was Ma Hutchin. Herbert depended upon her for the daily running of the Home and the attention to individual children. He could supply leadership, inspiration and vision. He could walk into the Home and take the prayers, play games, have a chat with the older children, read the riot act if necessary. But Herbert could not have faced staying in the Home all day, ordering the food, planning the menus, nursing the sick ones, sorting out the petty squabbles and so on. In short, the Home could not have functioned without Ma Hutchin. Herbert depended upon her both to run it and also to free him to evangelise outside.

The Children's Home and Mission was established because Herbert White possessed an independence that made him bold

The Evangelist

enough to take risks. Yet he relied upon two extraordinary
women who were blessed both with the abilities he lacked and
also with the graciousness to accept his dependence upon
them.

Herbert's character was marked by contradictory features.
He was partly an independent, Victorian entrepreneur who
thrust himself forward, confident that all would be well.
Yet, almost simultaneously, he could shun the limelight,
worry intensely, lean upon others and develop modern
concepts. These complexities do not lessen his standing or
achievements. They do demonstrate the internal struggles he
must have experienced and do explain some of his swings in
moods and actions. In many ways, he is a reflection of
Elijah in the Old Testament. Elijah suddenly emerges as a
mighty man of God who strides alone into the presence of the
evil King Ahab, who condemns wickedness, who defeats the
prophets of Baal in a public contest and who then, in high
excitement, runs for miles through pouring rain. Yet soon
after, the same Elijah is in fear and flight and is so
depressed that he wants to die. He then has to find God not
in the noisy earthquake but "in the soft whisper of a
voice." [4] Like Elijah, Herbert experienced mighty victories
which stimulated noisy praise. Yet these could be followed
by anti-climax, a heaviness and almost a withdrawal. It was
still the same man. Perhaps, as with Elijah, the down-side
served as a corrective. The fears, anxieties and depression
stopped any tendency to over confidence, to reliance on his
own great gifts, to self-promotion. The withdrawal turned
him to "the soft whisper of a voice", to listening to and
speaking with God. The apparently conflicting sides of
Herbert thus really kept his extremes in balance and
developed his personality as a rounded whole.

COMPASSION AND COMMUNICATION

Other characteristics of Herbert White were more straight forward yet no less interesting for they contribute to an understanding of what he was like. From his early days, he conveyed a deep compassion for children in need. This outstanding trait may have been stimulated by the loss of his own mother when he was 16. Certainly he always felt an empathy with children who lacked proper care. On one occasion, a woman came to the door of the Home with a small girl. The Home was full to overflowing but Herbert's solution was for the girl to sleep in the same bed as Edith while he bedded down in the office. The next day another bed was provided anonymously. His compassion continued once children were in the Home and he was deeply moved by their sickness or handicaps and would go to great lengths to obtain expert treatment, hospitalisation or convalescence. The concern then continued after they left the Home. Peter Kemp was badly wounded in France during the war and shipped to a hospital in Britian. Within a few hours, Herbert was at the bedside where, in the ward, he knelt and prayed for him. Herbert and some of his family continued to make the long trips to Manchester to visit him regularly. Peter relapsed on to the danger list but then recovered and was discharged. When he arrived on crutches, at a London station, Herbert was waiting and took him to Tiptree to rest. No wonder Peter later said, "He was a good friend and most helpful to me at a difficult time." Peter's experience is more dramatic than most. More typical are the many letters to Herbert (and Edith and Ma) from former children thanking them for years of kindness, care and love. One wrote in 1950 of Herbert as "a father who would scan the streets all night for a lost boy, and freely forgive some blatant hooliganism... In sickness and sadness there was always someone who understood and sympathised."

Former children sometimes recalled how strict Herbert could be so it is timely to note that his discipline co-existed with compassion and kindness. As Jon Sweet put it, "He had that mixture.... You knew you were talking to someone who knew the ropes. He could be strict but he could be compassionate." To Herbert, control was a part of kindness. He believed that children required both discipline and love. And for over 50 years his heart was sensitive to the needs of deprived children.

The compassion was within Herbert from his early days. Another feature, his capacity to communicate with children, probably developed as the years went by. His approach seemed to be to act as an authority figure with the younger children while also giving some time to playing with them. The closer relationships he left to the sisters. Then, as they grew older, so he became closer to them. Peter Kemp described it well by saying that "As a young child I saw him from a distance" but then explaining how in his teens they would walk and converse together. He would often take the teenagers with him to open airs or to churches where he was preaching and, on the return trip, would open his heart. Several mentioned that, in these talks, Herbert would talk both about their futures and his. It was a shared giving which promoted communication. Herbert saw every child before they left the Home. There were points he made to almost every child - open a post office savings account, look for a secure job, don't mix with bad company, don't swear or gamble, do read the Bible everyday and go to church. In addition, he added advice specific to that youngster like "control your temper", "get up on time", "keep your clothes tidy". Then he would pray with them and assure them that the Home was still their home. Advice given from the old to the young is often like talking to the wind. Yet numbers of the former children later wrote back to say how his advice had remained with them. Youngsters will accept guidance from adults they love and respect. Dr. Martin Lloyd-Jones stated that Herbert's outstanding feature was "his loveable character. His face, his very demeanour, his whole deportment radiated love."[5]   Youngsters perceived this love and hence they communicated with Herbert.

Herbert's capacity to communicate with the younger generation must have been helped by his sense of humour. He was always ready to see the funny side of a situation. One day he was showing visitors around the home when they came to the sick bay of which Herbert was rather proud as it had just been re-decorated. Flinging open the door he saw a small boy sitting up in bed with a bowl of custard from which he was flicking yellow blobs on to the blue ceiling. Herbert should have reprimanded him but couldn't as he burst out laughing. Again, one day Herbert parked a car outside the Home and climbed out Bible in hand. An enormous crash stopped him in his tracks and he turned to discover that the engine had fallen completely out of the car on to the road. Children gathered around to hear him shouting, "Praise the Lord." When asked why he was praising, he retorted, "The Lord made sure I got home first and no one was hurt."[6] Subsequently he continued to joke with the children about the Rolls Royce he was expecting but remained content with his Hillman which he called "an answer to prayer on wheels." As his daughter Olive expressed it, Herbert was "full of fun", cracking corny jokes of the kind lapped up by small children and engaging in zany behaviour which appealed to teenagers.

Compassion, communication, humour were obvious parts of Herbert's make-up because they were revealed in everyday actions. There is one other feature which needs to be mentioned simply because he did not show it - Herbert never involved himself in local or national politics. Barnardo did, at times, lobby M.P.s for changes in legislation relating to children. General William Booth of the Salvation Army, without joining a political party, vigorously called for government action to reduce unemployment and poverty. While Herbert was building up the Home, not far away in Bow and Poplar another Christian, George Lansbury, was throwing in his lot with the new Labour Party. Lansbury was angered by the suffering caused by poverty, especially the suffering of children. His response was to become a local councillor where he participated in the bringing in of municipal housing, school meals and health clinics. Later, elected as an M.P., he served as a cabinet minister and then as leader of the Labour Party where he bravely, and on Christian grounds, campaigned for greater social justice. [7]

By contrast with Lansbury but in common with his admired Muller, Herbert White distanced himself from politics. In fact, some of his views and practices had radical implications. His readiness, along with other staff members, to take very low wages was a rejection of the prevailing belief that wage levels should be set by the market forces of demand and supply. Similarly, his views on loans and investments were unusual - very unusual for one who used to work in a bank. Under Herbert's influence, the Home would not borrow money and would not invest it to earn interest. The reasons stem partly from taking seriously the Biblical injunctions against usury: partly from the view - as explained by one of the trustees, James Stokes in 1948 that they should not gamble with God's money by investing it;[8] and partly from a belief that storing money away for interest implied a dependence upon money not God. The extra-ordinary nature of these economic practices can be underlined by noting that at the time the national child care societies relied heavily on returns from invested money. Indeed, in the same period when James Stokes was talking, the much larger Waifs and Strays Society (the Church of England Children's Society) was drawing in City men to re-organise its investment policies on more profitable lines.[9]

George Lansbury would have approved of the practice of some taking lower salaries for the good of all. He was opposed to the economic system whereby the rich increased their wealth merely by drawing interest on their investments. However, Lansbury worked for legislation to apply what he regarded as Christian principles to society for the good of all. Thus, through his party, he wanted to create more equal incomes, the abolition of poverty and an economic system not fuelled by selfish gain. Herbert, however, would have nothing to do with party politics. He applied his Christian views to the immediate Christian setting where he lived and worked. Probably his approach was along the lines that people had to be converted first and then a better society would automatically come about. There was one other factor. If Herbert had identified himself with a particular political stand-point he might have alienated some of the Home's Christian supporters. To him, the immediate well-being of the Home and its children came before any long-term benefits that might come from political involvement.

HERBERT AND THE HOME

Whatever Herbert's personality and character, child care students will assess him according to the quality of care provided by the Home to its children. However, any assessment of care is problematic partly because there is not universal agreement on what constitutes good care and partly because any criterion of care is difficult to measure. For instance, it might be accepted that one benchmark of care is whether a child has a good relationship with an adult in the Home. But just what is "a good relationship" and how is it to be measured? In the case of the Children's Home and Mission, these difficulties are magnified because the period under discussion is in the past.

In the face of such difficulties, attempts have been made in previous chapters to compare the Home with contemporary child care practice within the Poor Law and other voluntary children's societies. Here another gambit will be tried. As mentioned, the 1940s witnessed the publication of the Curtis and Clyde Reports. They gave particular attention to residential child care much of which was located within voluntary bodies. Curtis commented, "In the independent Homes there is much greater variety of standards, ranging from the very good to the definitely bad."[10] From the two reports, it is possible to identify nine factors which the committees used when making judgements about care. It thus becomes possible to assess, however crudely, the Home against these standards and to do so for the 1940s and 50s, the last period of Herbert's life.

1. The Family Model. The Curtis and Clyde Reports gave priority to the need for children's homes to model themselves on the nuclear family, to create a family atmosphere and structure. They were critical of large homes located in huge buildings where "the rooms were often bare and comfortless, and so large that it was usually impossible to set aside any place for quiet occupation or hobbies."[11] They praised smaller homes, or at least those larger ones which split their children into groups, because they were more akin to the family life experienced by most children.

It is as well to acknowledge that no children's home can be the same as the kind of private family in which two (or sometimes one) parents look after a small number of children to whom they are related. Judith Tell poignantly made this point when she recalled, in the 1930's, being "ill in bed with swollen glands and a sister came into the sick room and she brought me an Easter Egg. I felt like crying because it was affection." In most families, such a gift and attention would be taken for granted but it could not always be so in an institution. Again, Jon Sweet felt that he suffered an injustice at school when, apparently because a teacher took a dislike to him, he was not promoted to a higher class. Jon explained that he did not bother to ask the staff at the Home to take up his case whereas he would have asked parents. Jon was very appreciative of his time at the Home yet he added,

> "There are disadvantages: being treated *en mass*. I often felt I wanted to be treated as an individual in my own right and not as part of an institution. As a junior I enjoyed the country (at Tiptree), at a more senior age you need to feel your own

identity."

The Children's Home and Mission usually contained 60-80 children. This was not an enormous number by contemporary standards but it could hardly be a family with a small 'f'. Any judgement, therefore, must concern whether it did promote family features despite that in-built disadvantage.

To its credit, the Home always kept boys and girls under the same roof. If this seems an obvious part in any strategy to create the feel of a family then it should be noted that many children's homes were single sex. The Waifs and Strays Society did not endorse the policy of mixed homes until 1946 and still had some all girl homes in 1968.[12] Further, the children in the Home had long had individual lockers and possessions and, probably in the 1940s, had been allocated a particular staff member with whom to relate. During the 1940s and 50s they were allowed their own pets and enjoyed smaller bedrooms. It is not possible to say whether these improvements originated within the Home or were a response to suggestions from the Home Office inspector.

Efforts were made to create a family atmosphere and with some success. Keith White points out that there is only one instance of a boy and girl from within the Home marrying each other. Such an event was rare precisely because the children did regard each other as brothers and sisters. Judith Tell describes how, despite minor arguments common to all families, the children did relate closely to and did support one another. She said,

> "We were not moved around which was good. The children who came in after you tended to be younger so you moved up. We knew each other and were completely a family. If one person was upset we'd say 'Are you homesick? Come on you can be first at this game'. And it remains until this day. We are still friends. It is just like sisters and brothers. We were so close. We were

an absolute family to each other."

Other former residents also remark upon the family feeling, upon the lack of bullying, upon the very close links that developed between the children. As with Judith, these links often continued after they left the Home because they felt they were connected with the children they had grown up with on a long term basis. As one stated publicly in 1952,

> "This atmosphere of home and family life that Pa White fostered is something which every child needs to create a self-respect and to form a background which would be lacking otherwise."[13]

The speaker was stating what child care experts have often said, namely that children need to have a positive self image about themselves and that this tends to stem from being accepted as part of a family. Moreover, as Judith Tell perceptively observed, she and her friends later established successful families of their own because they had learnt both to make and value good family relationships. The Curtis and Clyde Reports took the establishment of a family model and the creation of a family atmosphere as a benchmark for children's homes and, in the present writer's assessment, the Children's Home and Mission would have met with their approval.

2. *Quality of Staff.* The maintenance of relationships which approximate to those of family life within a children's home depend very much upon the quality and quantity of its staff. The Curtis and Clyde Reports paid tribute to the devotion of many residential workers while regretting that a minority regarded their job merely as a means to a pay packet and a roof over their heads. They noted that few staff possessed qualifications in regard to the care of children and, indeed, that there was no nationally recognised qualification in residential care. Even more worrying were homes where too few staff cared for too many children often with the result of a high turnover

rate amongst demoralised workers. Putting the two reports together, it is seen that the best homes were considered to have a low staff/child ratio - of about one to seven - with staff capable of giving affection and understanding to children and enjoying job satisfactions as reflected in staff stability. The worst ones were those with high ratios - up to one staff for seventeen children - with disinterested and disaffected workers characterised by a high turn-over rate.

The Home at Woodford possessed few if any staff with child care or social science qualifications. Certainly, Herbert had none. A few of the sisters came from nursing backgrounds but they were the exception. However, by the 1940s and 1950s, the Home did have the advantage of a good number of workers. In all, some 15 adults served about 70 children. Not counting those, like Edith, who dealt mainly with administrative matters, the ratio still averaged one care worker to six or seven children. It is difficult to evaluate just how affectionate and understanding they were. Some former children did consider that some sisters, howbeit friendly and helpful, did keep a certain distance from them in order to avoid being too emotionally involved or to avoid the charge of having favourites. Clearly, other staff members, like Ma Hutchin, were able to display affection without favouritism and were understanding of the needs of individual children, particularly the homesick, ill and lonely ones. They thus stimulated responses of respect, affection, even love. One point is certain. Staff turn-over was low. Particularly in the 1940s, a stability - remarkable for any children's home - was achieved.

3. Community Integration. The Curtis and Clyde Reports expressed a belief that children in residential homes should be a part of their local neighbourhoods. The Clyde committee criticised homes which were geographically isolated from communities. The Curtis committee criticised voluntary bodies in that "a far higher proportion of children were educated inside the Homes than in the local authority establishments."[14] Apart from the temporary sojourn in Tiptree, the Children's Home and Mission remained in Woodford which, by the 1940s, was a busy, urban community. After the war, some consideration was given to staying at Tiptree. Interestingly, in making the decision to concentrate operations in Crescent Road, Herbert and his colleagues took into account the child care advantages of being within a lively neighbourhood rather than being isolated in the country. In regard to schooling, the Home had always sent its children outside of the premises and so to local schools where they mixed with other children. During the 1950s, the children were also encouraged to attend outside churches and organisations like the Boys Brigade. However, two criticisms can be made. One is that outside of school and church there seemed few links with local children, no going into their homes, no inviting them back to the Home. The other is that membership of outside organisations was mainly with religious bodies. The children did not appear to play for local football teams or attend secular youth clubs. The Curtis and Clyde committees would probably have approved of the geographical location of the Home and its integration into local schools. But they might well have considered its links with leisure facilities somewhat restrictive and contacts with outside families somewhat lacking.

4. Physical Standards. The two committees examined both diet and material standards in children's homes. They found, generally, that most children received sufficient food although sometimes lacking in variety. However, the Clyde Report did mention a few voluntary homes where meals were so skimpy that the children were consequently tired and listless. Material standards gave more cause for concern. The best homes were well decorated, spacious, and with areas set aside for leisure facilities. The worst had peeling paint, dirty floors, needed repairs and contained no separate play areas.

How did the Home measure up to these standards? During its

early years, the menu at the Home was just about sufficient.
But an improvement occurred in the 1940s and 50s. The
acquisition of Tiptree ensured a supply of home grown
vegetables and fruit. The growing number of churches which
supported the Home also meant a steady supply of gifts in
kind. The church which I attended in Ilford always gave its
Harvest Thanksgiving produce to the Home and this included
not just fruit and vegetables but also tea, coffee, rice
(Herbert would be pleased), tizer and lemonade. The amount
of food and the variety of the menus in the 1950s would have
amazed the children of previous generations.

The physical state of the Home was always well maintained.
Herbert was no "do it yourself type" but he considered it a
Christian duty to look after the property. Ma Hutchin
ensured that high standards of cleanliness were kept inside
the Home. After the war, the Home received war damage
compensation and this ensured that the buildings were in
good condition when the children returned from Tiptree.
Most important, as Mr Tod noted, the children enjoyed ample
and separate play space both indoors and out. Soon
improvements were made to the dining area by partitioning it
off and so making it more compact. The physical standards
of the Home would have satisfied any inspectors.

5. *Leisure Activities.* Space for leisure was not
sufficient. The Curtis and Clyde Reports were insistent
that children's homes should also provide children with the
encouragement, time and equipment to enjoy their recreation.
Their ire was particularly directed at institutions which
loaded so many household duties on children that leisure was
almost squeezed out. In the worst places, children were
made to devote four hours a day to cleaning, scrubbing,
polishing and sweeping. The committees were of the opinion
that children should participate in household tasks but not
more than half an hour per day. Priority should be given to
their hobbies and play capped by an annual holiday.

By the 1950s, the Home had reduced the amount of time

children spent on household jobs. Probably only the older girls devoted more than half an hour to such work and here the justification was that they were being trained for future employment. However, even this emphasis declined as wider job opportunities opened up. Recreation was encouraged with the hobbies of stamp collecting, chess and pet-keeping being popular indoors while football, cricket, rounders and netball in seasonal vogue outside. It is difficult to obtain information on what toys were available although the lack of recollections suggests they were not in abundance. One fact is certain. The children continued to enjoy a number of day trips to the country and seaside while an annual holiday had become part of the yearly cycle.

6. *Religion* The majority reports of the Curtis and Clyde committees argued that religion should be an integral part of life within children's homes. They wanted religion which was interesting and relevant to everyday life. The Clyde Report added "Where possible children should attend a church outside the Home."[15] The least desirable scenario occurred where religious teaching was boring, dry, irrelevant and restricted to within the institution.

The Woodford children usually attended a church and often a Sunday School outside the Home. Within the Home, Herbert might have gone on too long in some of his talks but they were rarely boring and usually relevant. His was a Christianity which, sometimes literally, prayed for and received the daily bread. Judith Tell remembered his ability to make Bible stories come alive saying, "He could go on for ages but I always enjoyed it. I thrilled to it."

The Home's Christianity, however, did not just stem from Herbert. Former children also explained that they were impressed by the sisters and Ma Hutchin. These women spoke less frequently about their faith yet displayed it in their patience and kindness. Interestingly, the Home Office inspector, Robert Tod, said that before going to the Home he viewed its religious reputation with some trepidation.

Later he perceived it as a positive factor which offered children both the ethical principles on which to base their lives and also a strength with which to keep them.

7. *Medical Care.* Children in institutions are known to be more vulnerable to illness and disease. The Curtis and Clyde Reports were therefore in concert that adequate and regular medical care should be available to them. Interestingly, the very large children's homes, for all their other disadvantages, often did have resident medical staff. The very small homes, for all their advantages, sometimes had tenuous links with medical practitioners.

Medical care is one criterion on which there can be no doubt that the Home in Woodford would have rated highly. During this period, they had up to three general practitioners on hand. They always examined any new arrivals to the Home and dealt immediately with any requests. Further, the children also had the services of a dentist and chiropodist.

8. *Contacts with Relatives.* The Curtis and Clyde committees urged that, unless there were good reasons to the contrary, children in public care should be kept in touch with their natural families. They condemned staff who considered that parents who had "failed" their children should be discouraged from seeing them. Such an attitude both harmed the children and also lessened any chances of re-uniting the family.

As mentioned before, Herbert and his staff early on put aside time when parents could visit the Home. Gradually the approach changed from one of controlled visits to one of encouragement of contact. Of course some of the children were orphans. Others did lose touch with their relatives. But the evidence from the former children who were interviewed is that, where possible, contact was facilitated with the children often going out for a day or spending a holiday with relatives. Although the staff of the Home had no formal training in child care, their attitude to the

importance of parental involvement was probably in advance
of most other residential establishments of the time.

9. *After-Care*   Children who spent their childhoods in pre-
war Poor Law institutions found that, when they were 14 or
15 years old, they were required to leave and that was that.
The institutions had no obligation to spend further money on
them or to maintain contact. No wonder that numbers soon
found it difficult if not impossible to cope outside. To be
sure, some public and voluntary bodies adopted the more
humane approach of encouraging leavers and the Curtis and
Clyde committees took up this point to explain that good
child care entailed some support for children after they
left residential homes.

If marks were awarded for keeping in touch with former
residents, then the Home at Woodford would have scored
highly. From the very beginning, leavers were told that the
Home was still theirs, were encouraged to visit and made
welcome if they came back for a few days. The Links
magazine is full of letters from children who maintained
contact. The 1940 edition contained one from an old boy and
his wife expressing appreciation that they had spent the
last 25 Christmases at the Home. They wrote, "The warm
welcome that we always receive and the trouble you all take
to make us happy and comfortable is equal to the best that
any parents could do for their children." The 1950 issue
carried a report of a re-union and a photo of a Mr W.
Cowling who was quoted as saying, "I have been back to the
Home every Christmas since 1911 and I do this because I was
happy at the Home. I think it is the best in existence and
it is well and truly a Home, not just an institution."

These and many other examples indicate that after-care, or
keeping in touch, was taken very seriously by the staff at
the Home. Such after-care was important for four reasons.
First, it allowed leavers to take on independence gradually.
To leave a settled abode for digs, a hostel, a live-in job,
even to go back to relatives, was unsettling and

challenging. The staff at the Home were open to the leavers to call back frequently in their early days when they most needed support. Second, it facilitated help in times of trouble, when isolation was experienced, a job lost, a relationship broken off, or when digs were needed. Third, it meant that parent figures were available at important formal occasions. The staff were frequently invited to and went to baptisms, 21st birthdays, weddings, dedication of babies. Fourth, it provided the former children with roots. All human beings need to know how and where they spent their childhoods, need to have some continuity with their past. Some ex residents maintained regular links. No doubt some lost them altogether. But the doors were always ready to be opened and sometimes contacts were resumed after many years. Harry Race took 60 years to do so. Finally, with his wife, he made the trip to Woodford and walked down Crescent Road. He said, "I saw two houses at the end with Have Faith in God written over them. I wondered if it was now private housing. The door opened and Victor White came down and said 'Are you looking for somebody?' I said 'Yes. I used to live here.' He looked at me and said, 'You've come home.'"

One former boy expressed some ambivalence about continually identifying with the Home. He said,

> "I owe the staff so much and they contributed so much to my life, more than I can ever say or repay. At the same time, to return arouses in me feelings which go way back and which I don't want aroused. I don't want to be seen as an Old Boy. Life has moved on and I'm a person in my own right. I can't go back without feeling the boy again - uncomfortably so. The role of the parent is to prepare the child to leave them. Parents can't continue to keep their children."

His feelings, so well and honestly recorded, were not found amongst other interviewees. He felt the more strongly because he had been able to find a fulfilling life with which the Home, naturally enough, wished to identify. As he wisely said, parents should prepare children for independence but this should not entail the cessation of contact. Rather it means continuing a relationship while accepting that the former child has grown up. My judgement is that the Home staff did offer more regular contact in the years immediately following a child leaving the Home. The contact grew less after that although with the door always open. Such was good after-care.

By the 1950s, the best children's homes probably contained no more than 20 children who were cared for by stable staff capable of making sensitive relationships within a family atmosphere: the homes would provide adequate diet, material standards and medical care along with ample opportunities for leisure: such homes would be integrated into the local communities: children would be encouraged to maintain links with their relatives: in terms of religion, the aim would be to present but not impose an interesting and relevant faith: leaving the homes would be regarded not as a final break but as one step towards independence.

Certainly, the Children's Home and Mission did not measure up to all these criteria. Yet it did well on most of them and probably would have been accepted by the Curtis and Clyde committees. The 1950s witnessed much public criticism of children's homes which were frequently seen as being too institutionalised, too impersonal, lacking in affection and purpose, and having too few staff. Such condemnation could not be levelled at the Home. Interestingly, the standards within the Home were reached not after training in child care and not, apparently, from intensive study of contemporary child care literature. Rather they sprang from the coming together, under Herbert and Ma's leadership, of a group of people, highly motivated to care for deprived children, who regarded their service as a Christian vocation which entailed providing the best possible environment for them and whose understanding of young people tended to be drawn from their own personal experiences and from Biblical insights into the needs of children.

MAN OF FAITH

This book has depicted Herbert White as the founder of a children's home which provided satisfactory care for hundreds of children over a fifty year period. This achievement is attributed partly to the competent staff around him and partly to his own skills and personality. Yet all his skills and all his complex traits of character were secondary to and moulded by one other factor. He was a man of faith.

Faith in what? Not faith in a church. Herbert remained in membership at the Baptist church but denomination never meant a great deal to him. As he said, "There will be no labels in heaven." So what is faith? John White (no relative) clears the ground. "Faith is not a feeling. It is not even the feeling that something is going to happen in answer to our prayers." Instead, faith is "the obedient response of our wills to who God is and what he says." [16] In short, faith is exercised towards a person and that person is God. Herbert summed it up in the text which he had carved over the Home, "Have faith in God".

Herbert's fundamental faith was a belief in a God who existed as God the Father, God the Son, and God the Holy Spirit. But further, as George Carey - now the Archbishop of Canterbury - put it, "...in the Bible, faith rests in the character of God himself."[17] The character of God, according to Herbert, was of one both able and willing to meet the needs of Christians.

His faith, then, rested on the existence and nature of God and entailed obedience to that God. For Herbert, certain implications followed. One was that he sought to know as much as he possibly could about God. He did this through constant study of the Bible where he discovered both the objectives which Christians should be pursuing and examples of how faith should be exercised. At a meeting in 1948, he pointed to some of the prophets in the Old Testament and apostles in the New Testament as instances of people whose faith in God allowed them to carry out God's intentions. He added that the faith of contemporary Christians could only emulate these Biblical characters "if they do not live in sin and if they go on in believing prayer, until the answer is given." To Herbert White, the Bible was no out of date history book but a divinely inspired volume which taught people like himself how to exercise faith daily.

The next implication was prayer. If the nature of God was such that He was willing and able to provide for his children then it was the duty of Christians to make their needs known to Him through prayer. Noticeably, after Jesus gave the injunction "Have faith in God", He proceeded to teach about prayer.[18] Faith thus leads to prayer and Herbert's life was characterised by regular believing prayer. At the annual meeting of 1930, Herbert was reported as saying that, "They rejoiced to be able to tell out what God had done for them in answer to believing prayer. During the year they had had many difficulties to face, but God had brought them through triumphantly - in fact all through the 30 years of their existence they had had daily tests and found as they took everything to God in prayer that He under took and delivered."

The third implication was action. Knowing the nature of God, having sought his mind in the Scriptures, having presented his needs in prayer, Herbert then acted in expectation. The table would be set to await the arrival of food. The children would be got ready for the outing. The architect would be instructed to design the new hall. And so on for over 50 years.

The results of such faith were extraordinary. Without any publicity, without any requests to human agencies, the needs of staff, buildings, money, food, cars and holidays were always met. The sceptic might dismiss some incidents as coincidences. The baker just happened to have a surplus of buns when the Home had none. The arrival of an unsolicited cheque just happened to come when the Home was penniless. But coincidences do not occur continually for over half a century. The simple and more logical conclusion is that God did respond to the faith of His people.

Herbert had no doubt that God was responding and intervening directly to help the children. The outcome never failed to thrill him and the Home would echo with the sound of his praises. The repeated provision served to increase his faith and made him a Godly optimist. Mr James Stokes once stated that he would meet Herbert "perhaps twice or three time some weeks and we have a cup of coffee together after an open-air service in the City. Over these cups I hear little bits that perhaps you do not hear. But whatever may be the problem or the question, there is always this cheery thing at the end: 'Well, God has got something in store for us; He will see us through'. That is the dynamic of this work."[19] Despite occasional lows, Herbert's prevailing mood was one of happy expectation. As Peter Kemp recalled, he would laughingly declare "how wealthy he was, the son of the most wealthy person in the world - yet he hadn't got a penny in the bank."

He would not say so himself but there was something Christ-like in Herbert's attitudes. For the Christ himself had a faith that his Father would enable him to triumph over evil: the Christ himself held few if any possessions yet never wavered in his confidence that his needs would be met. Perhaps it was because he trod the same path that Herbert sometimes glowed with the qualities of Christ. As the Rev. Parkinson of the Woodford Baptist Church said, in 1930, if a spiritual photograph was taken of Herbert White then the presence of Jesus would always be seen standing beside him.[20]

I have played cricket for over 50 years. Once a year I go

to a test match to watch some of the greatest players in the world. Sometimes their feats and skills make me feel so hopeless by comparison that I might as well give up playing. One of the dangers of viewing Herbert's great faith and faithfulness is to make us feel so inferior as to be discouraged. It is a bit like the reaction of Peter to Jesus, "Go away from me, Lord. I am a sinful man."[21] At this juncture some of Dr. Martyn Lloyd-Jones' reflections upon Herbert's life are helpful. He points out that, according to 1 Corinthians 12, Christians are given various kinds of gifts of which one is faith. He explains that all Christians possess "saving faith" but, in addition, there is "a special gift which is given by the Holy Spirit to certain individuals within the Church to trust God implicitly, directly, and in simple manner....(it) is this remarkable and astonishing gift which has been given to our friend, Mr White, and which he has exercised for the past fifty long years."[22] Lloyd-Jones went on that other Christians have different gifts. So far from being discouraged, they should rejoice and be encouraged that God continues to give the gift of faith to the likes of Herbert White.

As early as 1911, Herbert declared, "Without money or influence or power we simply obeyed Him, and have found during this long test 'That He is faithful that promised'." So Herbert's life should be an inspiration to other Christians. We are not necessarily called to run a children's home on faith lines. Indeed, Lloyd-Jones warned that "There is always a danger that people should set out to try to imitate Mr White" with an outcome of disaster. Rather, like Herbert, we are required to "obey Him". The encouragement is that if we trust God, if we seek his will for our lives, if we exercise the gifts He gives us, in short if we obey Him, then all will be well even if we lack money, influence or power.

TODAY

Over 40 years have passed since Herbert White's death. Able, enthusiastic and committed leaders took over in the persons of Victor and Margaret White and then their son Keith and wife Ruth. Today's work occurs in very different social circumstances from that of the 1950s. The demand for residential care has fallen markedly. Improved material standards and more comprehensive welfare services have enabled more parents to cope with their own children. It is true that the last decade and a half has witnessed a marked increase in both inequality and poverty. For instance, between 1979-91 average income rose by 35 per cent but for the bottom tenth of the population it dropped by 14 per cent. The number dependent upon incomes of Income Support level or below (usually considered as the poverty line) has doubled in this period. [23] It is also true that children looked after by public authorities are once again predominantly the children of poor parents. However, the majority of these children are placed either in foster care or supervised in their own homes or with relatives. The decline in residential establishments has been particularly characteristic of voluntary societies.

The Children's Home and Mission, like other voluntary bodies, has had to adapt and change. It is now called Mill Grove and its residential component, although still thriving, is numerically much smaller and is just one aspect of the work. Mill Grove also supports a play group for the neighbourhood, contains a school for children with acute learning difficulties, stimulates local community action and sponsors the Christian Child Care Network which links families with difficulties to Christian agencies and helpers. Yet, despite the changes, there are clear links with the past. At a time when children's homes are often criticised, Mill Grove's residential care is positive, multi-cultural and flexible. Its young people are well integrated into the neighbourhood and particularly participate in organised sport and recreation. A high proportion have done well at school and, amongst its present leavers, all have found jobs. It thus continues the high standards, the emphasis on securing employment for older children and the development of recreational, educational and spiritual life - the whole person - which was established by Herbert White. The sense of mission also remains with both Victor and Keith in demand as speakers and with the latter a well-known writer and lecturer in social welfare circles. The near future will see the publication of a new NIV Bible drawn from the experiences of prayers amongst the members of Mill Grove. Not least, the church at Abridge still grows and has just built a manse for its minister. The changes are thus within a framework of continuity which itself stems from an abiding loyalty to the Christian principles upon which Herbert White and Rosa Huchin started the Home.

Despite the continuity at Woodford, it can not be denied that social welfare in general is undergoing enormous economic, moral and institutional changes. Does this mean that the example of Herbert White and his colleagues is irrelevant to today? Far from it. As a Christian who has spent most of his working life in the world of social welfare, I consider that much of what Herbert stood for and lived by is needed today.

Herbert, along with Ma and others, felt a strong sense of social obligation, towards those in need. He could have chosen to promote his own career and interests by staying with the bank where his undoubted talents would have secured him a high position, large income and safe pension. Outside of work, he could have focused most of his attention on his own family. Instead, his sense of obligation towards others led him in a different direction. Michael Schluter and David Lee in their profound book *The R Factor* explain that in Britian individualism has become a God.[24] The prevailing philosophy is that individuals should seek their own self-interests. It is seen in individuals who neglect their own elderly parents. It is seen in an increasingly affluent population who care little for the poor. Even amongst Christians, there are those who are content to live in comfortable security far from those who face the social deprivations, the difficulties, the over-crowding, the lack of amenities in the inner cities and sprawling housing estates. The result, as Schluter and Lee point out, is a society increasingly divided not just by income, wealth and opportunities but also by geographical distance. They argue the thesis that Britain's population has lost its sense of social obligation. My opinion is that it is not completely dead but I agree that the social and spiritual problems of our day will not be tackled until far more people accept obligations towards others - just as Herbert White did.

Next, Herbert was not materialistic. He was not concerned whether he owned a suit of clothes let alone a house. He refused to use for his own purpose any money donated to the Home. The gifts that were directed to the Whites provided the family with an income sufficient for their modest needs - but no more.

Today materialism is an accepted, even highly regarded, trait. Possessions, be they cars, clothes, computers, furniture, hi-fi equipment, second homes, investments, have become ends in themselves. Even in the sphere of welfare, directors of Social Services Departments and large voluntary societies may take £50,000 a year, job perks and a large pension in order to run services for society's most needy and poorest members. My view is that materialism as an end in itself and material possessions accumulated while others are lacking are social evils. The Biblical teaching is that material wealth can be a barrier between people and God. Even amongst those who claim no alleigance to God, materialism can become more important than personal relationships and more important than social justice.

Herbert White did not disregard material things. He wanted shelter, food, recreation, holidays for the children. He wanted them to obtain employment with adequate incomes. But he was never possessed by materialism. He never regarded the acquisition of money, possessions, security, as the main motive in human functioning. In short, he did not consider things more sacred than people. Above all, he insisted that the things of the spirit were more real and lasting than those of metal, wood, stone and plastic. I live in an area of much poverty and I long that its residents should have their fair share of dry housing, good food, job opportunities and adequate incomes, for all these material matters are a part of God's creation. But I also believe that material things should be our servants not our masters. They should be mere tools which we use to enjoy relationships with others and with God. Herbert White not only held this view, he put it into practice.

Lastly, Herbert White located himself amongst those he wished to serve. He did not run the Home from a distance. He did not just visit the children. He did not appeal for funds to meet their needs while living in affluence himself. Perhaps he took as an example the Christ who left heaven not to dwell in a palace amongst the powerful but to locate himself with the ordinary people, close to the prostitutes, the lepers, the beggars and the oppressed.

Today responsibility for the care of many needy people is placed upon central government and local authority agencies supplemented by national voluntary organisations. Unfortunately, as these agencies have grown in size and influence, so a social and physical distance has developed between the helpers and the helped. Directors and managers of services now rarely live in the inner cities and council schemes where so many of the people who knock on the doors of their agencies dwell. From comfortable offices they make policy decisions about citizens whom they rarely meet. Even children's homes are increasingly run by staff who do not live on the premises. My experience and observations lead me to the conclusion that this distancing has unfortunate outcomes. The knowledge upon which policy makers make decisions is often second hand: they can not fully understand the users of services if they do not know them. Further, it perpetuates social divisions, splitting people between well-off professionals and low-income clients, between givers and recipients, the powerful and the powerless, the outsiders and the locals. I long for a more cohesive society in which welfare agencies belong to, are responsive to and are even run by and from within, the communities they are meant to serve. Herbert White so located himself amongst the needy that not only did he share himself with them but also their needs became his needs.

A strong sense of social obligation, a rejection of materialism, an acceptance of locating himself amongst those he served. These characteristics of Herbert White may have gone out of fashion. More's the pity. As I have tried to explain elsewhere, I believe that a just society must be built upon citizens who accept responsibilities for each other, upon a sharing of possessions which springs from a recognition that all people are of equal value to God, and upon welfare services which bind people together. [25] Herbert White has much to teach us today.

THE BEING OF GOD

Herbert improved the life of hundreds of children. His principles and practises have much to offer to today's social services. But he was more than that. As Dr. Martyn Lloyd-Jones put it,

> "A work like this is a proof in and of itself of the Being of God. You cannot explain this work apart from God. You cannot explain the astonishing miracles and happenings that have taken place in connection with it, the wonderful answers to prayer - they cannot be explained adequately, and in any other terms, apart from the Being of God."[26]

In the Old Testament, many chapters end with words like

those of Ezekiel 37, "Then they will know that I am the Lord". In many ways, Herbert stands out like those Old Testament figures whose steadfast faith convinces others that there is a Lord God. We should rejoice in Herbert's faith but more we should rejoice in the existence and nature of the God in whom he had faith.

In other ways, particularly his generosity, his zeal, his evangelism, and his failings, Herbert is a reminder of the New Testament disciples like Peter. Further, his compassion, his self-sacrifice, his steadfastness, his faithfulness, are even a reflection of the Christ. Herbert would not have claimed that comparison for himself but he would have been delighted if anything in himself pointed others to the Son of God. As he wrote in 1924,

"I want to please my Lord
And do what he shall say,
That others may take note that I
Have been with Him today.
So shall His cause be spread
Wherever I may be,
And Jesus' name be glorified
Till He shall come for me."

References

1. *Links,* 1952,p.59
2. A.Gammie, *William Quarrier,* Pickering & Inglis, 1937,pp.170-71.
3. K. White, *A Place for Us,* Mill Grove, 1976,pp.110-11.
4. 1 Kings 19 verse 12, Good News Bible.
5. *Links,* 1952,p.10
6. K.White, *op.cit.,* p.108.
7. B.Holman, *Good Old George: The Life of George Lansbury,* Lion,1990.
8. *Links,* 1948,p.25.
9. J Stroud, *13 Penny Stamps,* Hodder and Stoughton, 1971,p.228.
10. *Report of the Care of Children Committee,* (Curtis Report), H.M.S.O.,1946,para 228.
11. *Op.cit.,* para 230.
12. J. Stroud, *op.cit.,* p.237.
13. *Links,* 1952,p.53.
14. Curtis Report, *op.cit.,* para 250.
15. *Report of the Committee on Homeless Children,* (Clyde Report), para 95.
16. J. White, *Greater Than Riches,* Inter-Varsity Press, 1992,p.134.
17. G. Carey in *The Lion Handbook of Christian Belief,* Lion, 1982, p.334.
18. Mark 11, verses 22-26.
19. *Links,* December 1928,p.6.
20. *Links,* December 1930,p.7.
21. Luke 5 verse 8.
22. *Links,* 1950.p.13.
23. See P. Alcock, *Understanding Poverty,* Macmillan, 1993.
24. M.Schluter and D. Lee, *The R Factor,* Hodder and Stoughton, 1993.
25. B. Holman, *A New Deal for Social Welfare,* Lion, 1993.
26. *Links,* 1950,pp.14-15.